POPE FRANCIS

T0372401

This volume is about Pope Francis, the diplomat. In his eight years of pontificate, Pope Francis as a peacemaker has propagated the ideas of human and divine co-operation to build a global human fraternity through his journeys outside the Vatican. This book discusses his endeavours to connect and develop a common peaceful international order between countries, faith communities, and even antagonistic communities through a peaceful journey of human beings.

The book analyses his speeches, and meetings as a diplomat of peace, including his visits to Cuba and the United States, and his mediations for peace in Colombia, Myanmar, Kenya, Egypt, Turkey, Jordan, Jerusalem, the Central African Republic, Sri Lanka, and Bangladesh. It discusses the role of Pope Francis as mediator in different circumstances through his own writings, letters, and Vatican documents; his encounters with world leaders; as well as his contributions to a universal understanding on inter-faith dialogue, climate change and the environment, and human migration and the refugee crisis. The volume also sheds light on his ideas on a post-pandemic just social order, as summarised in his 2020 encyclical.

A definitive work on the diplomacy and the travels of Pope Francis, this volume will be of great interest to scholars and researchers of religious studies, peace and conflict studies, ethics and philosophy, and political science and international relations. It will be of great interest to the general reader as well.

Mario I. Aguilar is Professor of Religion and Politics at the School of Divinity, St Mary's College, University of St Andrews, United Kingdom. A few of his recent publications include *Church, Liberation and World Religions: Towards a Christian–Buddhist Dialogue* (2012); *Pope Francis: His Life and Thought* (2014); *Christian Ashrams, Hindu Caves, and Sacred Rivers: Christian–Hindu Monastic Dialogue in India 1950–1993* (2016); *The Way of the Hermit: Inter-faith Encounters in Silence and Prayer* (2017); and *Interreligious Dialogue and the Partition of India: Hindus and Muslims in Dialogue about Violence and Forced Migration* (2018). His research interests include the study of religion; religion in the contemporary world; theology in Latin America and Africa; contextual theology; biblical studies and anthropology; Islam in Africa; the history of Tibet and Tibetan Buddhism; Christian–Buddhist dialogue; Hinduism, particularly monasticism in India; Christian–Hindu dialogue; and Hindu texts.

PEACEMAKERS
Series Editor: **Ramin Jahanbegloo**, *Executive Director of the Mahatma Gandhi Centre for Nonviolence and Peace Studies and the Vice-Dean of the School of Law at Jindal Global University, India*

Peace is one of the central concepts in the spiritual and political life of humanity. Peace does not imply the absence of war. It implies harmony, justice and empathy. Empathy is the key to education of peace in our world. In other words, despite the vast differences of values between cultures and traditions, it is still possible to grasp an understanding of one another, by 'empathy'. Throughout centuries, peacemakers have endorsed a 'shared human horizon' which according to them had the critical force of avoiding moral anarchy and relativism while acknowledging the plurality of modes of being human.

Today in a different manner and in a changed tone, but with the same moral courage and dissenting voice, this series on 'Peacemakers' offers the first comprehensive engagement with the problems of peace in our age, through a meticulous and thorough study of the lives and thoughts of peacemakers of all ages.

THE 14TH DALAI LAMA
Peacekeeping and Universal Responsibility
Mario I. Aguilar

NELSON MANDELA
Peace through Reconciliation
Neera Chandhoke

For more information about this series, please visit: www.routledge.com/Peacemakers/book-series/PCMK

POPE FRANCIS

Journeys of a Peacemaker

Mario I. Aguilar

Routledge
Taylor & Francis Group

LONDON AND NEW YORK

First published 2022
by Routledge
2 Park Square, Milton Park, Abingdon, Oxon OX14
4RN

and by Routledge
605 Third Avenue, New York, NY 10158

*Routledge is an imprint of the Taylor & Francis
Group, an informa business*

British Library Cataloguing-in-Publication Data
A catalogue record for this book is available from the
British Library

Library of Congress Cataloging-in-Publication Data
A catalog record has been requested for this book

ISBN: 978-0-367-75699-4 (hbk)
ISBN: 978-1-032-00023-7 (pbk)
ISBN: 978-1-003-17234-5 (ebk)

DOI: 10.4324/9781003172345

Typeset in Sabon
by codeMantra

THIS WORK IS DEDICATED TO
GLENDA TELLO

CONTENTS

ACKNOWLEDGEMENTS

Every book starts as an open canvass in which colours are added until the author is satisfied with the result. More so in the case of works about a religious leader and a globalised person, in this case my own portrait of Pope Francis. Pope Francis as the bishop of Rome has been an example of an ongoing peacemaker in the areas of sociopolitical conflict as well as in the spiritual areas of interreligious dialogue, and engagement with conflicts provoked by religious sectarianism. I have followed very closely his journeys, speeches, and meetings as one of his biographers, and my first acknowledgement goes to him as an example of a committed Christian who has moved hearts and peoples towards peace, understanding, and a real commitment to the poor and marginalised of this world.

This work was written and completed within the COVID-19 pandemic of 2020–2021 which I lived for the most part in isolation at Nalanda Hermitage in Santiago, Chile. My gratitude to the Routledge series editor Professor Ramin Jahanbegloo who not only commissioned this work but became an intellectual companion through our attendance of the Friday meetings of Scholars at the Peripheries, a group of Global South Scholars which I founded with scholars in Asia, Africa, and Latin America. Indeed, Pope Francis has been a shepherd of the peripheries during his pontificate and during his years of pastoral work in his native Argentina. I acknowledge the enormous efforts of librarians and archivists who over the past eight years have helped me with documents and manuscripts available at the Vatican, Argentina, Chile, India, Iraq, the European Union, and the United Kingdom.

I dedicate this work to my Life Companion, without whom despair would have been a reality during the pandemic. Even when I stayed on my own most of the time, channels of communication remained open and I acknowledge the companionship of Sara Aguilar, Dr Eve Parker, Dr James Morris, Dr Gordon T. Barclay, and Dr Ann Simpson. Parts of this work were sharpened by conversations with members of Laudato Si' International and Fundación Milarepa Chile as well as seminar presentations at the Centre for the Study of Religion and Politics (CSRP) of the University of St Andrews, Scotland, where I had the ongoing support of Dr Eric Stoddart and Professor Sabine Hyland. My personal gratitude to those who spent hours conversing with me about specific parts of Pope Francis' impact on the world of peacemakers and within non-Christian religions, including among many others Omar Mohammed and Angela Boskovitch (Mosul, Iraq, Rome, Paris), Hilary Chan (St. Andrews), Anupama Ranawana (Sri Lanka), Dr Camila Foncea, Jorge Cuché, and Ivonne Bell (Chile), Carolina Sanz, Ivón Cepeda, and Ángel Méndez (Mexico), Marcela Arévalo (Colombia), Shruti Dixit, Ishita Mahajan, Elilo Ezung, Elias Rathiulung, and Raj Bharat Patta (India), Arvin Gouw (Indonesia), Dr Calida Chu and Gillian Chu (Hong Kong), Dr Jama Musse Jama (Somaliland), and Patricia Palazzo Tsai (Brazil).

Mario I. Aguilar

Nalanda Hermitage, Santiago, Chile, on the 8th year of Pope Francis' pontificate (A.D. 2021).

SERIES EDITOR'S PREFACE

Peace is one of the central concepts of the spiritual and political life of humanity. When we study the world's religious and philosophical teachings, whether they are from the East or the West, we see that one of the basic ideals of all religions is peace. Peace does not imply simply absence of war. It implies harmony, justice, and empathy. Empathy is the key to education of peace in our world. In other words, despite the vast differences of values between cultures and traditions, it is still possible to grasp an understanding of one another, by 'empathy'. Therefore, we can maintain that all cultures have a shared core of common humanity. Throughout centuries, peacemakers endorsed a 'shared human horizon' which according to them had the critical force of avoiding moral anarchy and relativism while acknowledging the plurality of modes of being human. As a matter of fact, the first step for peacemakers has always been to not only assume that there are differences among nations, cultures, and traditions of thought but also to admit that people may have different value systems which need to be understood and approached dialogically and critically. Philosophy of peace is, thus, expressed here in the idea of a "self-respecting" community or nation which strives to remove its own imperfections instead of necessarily judging others. As a result, peacemaking is not only a call to cultivate humility but also to foster pluralism. Such a view is essential if we are to avoid the danger of cultural conformity and move towards the recognition of shared values of humanity and the acceptance of what Martin Luther King, Jr. called the 'cosmic companionship'. Put differently, it would be an error on our part to hope that we can achieve a truly universal vision of peace without an intercultural approach to the idea of civilisation. Peacemakers have always been in favour of a farsighted peacemaking in our world which has seriously advocated the logic of solidarity and civic friendship beyond national selfishness and global exclusion. Let us not forget that all peacemakers, either man or woman, young or old, from the West or the East, were engaged in the process of peace-seeking by fighting for care, openness, and empathy as constructive forms of being together. Today in a different manner and in a changed tone, but with the same moral courage and dissenting voice, this series on 'Peacemakers' offers the first comprehensive engagement with the problems of peace in our age, through a meticulous and thorough study of the lives and thoughts of peacemakers of all ages.

Ramin Jahanbegloo

INTRODUCTION

The choice of global peacemaking

On 13 March 2013, Cardinal Jorge Bergoglio, Archbishop of
Buenos Aires, was elected as the successor of Pope Benedict
XVI who had resigned previously.[1] It could be argued that the
Catholic Church was in a deep crisis of ungovernability, a central factor that triggered Benedict XVI's resignation.[2] Immediately after his election, Cardinal Bergoglio, the cardinal from the
ends of the world, was presented at St Peter's Square showing
a degree of warmth to those present and stressing his role as
the Bishop of Rome.[3] The choice of Archbishop Bergoglio as the
266th bishop of Rome pointed clearly to the cardinals' choice
of a leader coming from the periphery.[4] For the Bishop of Rome
within the Catholic Church takes precedence over all other bishops and becomes the centre of unity for those holding the teaching office, and de facto the leader of over 1 billion Catholics in
the world.[5] Bergoglio's portfolio included a clear leadership in
Argentina with a simplicity of life that made him pastorally close
to the poor and the marginalised, traditional and conservative in
his own spirituality, but a pioneer in dialogue with other Christians and non-Christians as well as a dissenting voice in politics
if needed.

In my previous work, one of the first to construct a history of
the Cardinal who became Pope Francis, I argued that his pastoral closeness to the poor would make a difference to the papacy
and that his spirituality would bring the Catholic Church to a

spiritual awakening.[6] However, at the time of Bergoglio's election in 2013 it was expected that because of his age and his own experience Pope Francis was not going to travel too far and too often as his predecessors, especially as John Paul II did. However, Pope Francis surprised a Catholic world over these years by engineering structural changes as important as those introduced by John XXIII and his calling of the Second Vatican Council. There is no doubt that Pope Francis has surprised us with his globalised sense of the world and his willingness to travel far to bring enemies together and to bring peace and understanding on the occasions in which he has been asked to support processes of national, regional, and global peacemaking. This work covers some of his peacemaking journeys from 2013 to 2021 and ends with Pope Francis' visit to Iraq in March 2021 within a global COVID-19 pandemic.[7]

It was during the 2020–2021 pandemic that Pope Francis played a significant role within the global community by performing global actions at times of despair. Examples of such global leadership were the global moment of prayer he led in St Peter's Square in March 2020, and his address to the 75th General Assembly of the United Nations on 25th September 2020. Pope Francis outlined the choices of a post-pandemic world, arguing that his option was 'the consolidation of multilateralism as the expression of a renewed sense of global co-responsibility, a solidarity grounded in justice and the attainment of peace and unity within the human family'.[8] Such option for multilateralism connected very clearly with the options for peace and universal responsibility outlined by the XIV Dalai Lama, and 'dismissed an emphasis on self-sufficiency, nationalism, protectionism, individualism and isolation'.[9] Such ideas had been already developed within Pope Francis' encyclical *Laudato Si'* (2015) when he externalised his own ideas on the 'common home'.[10] Those ideas were materialised in his calling for an Amazonian Synod through which he could carry out a consultation on his concerns for the 'common home' and the need to understand creation, ecology, and the stewardship of creation together. His reflections on such Synod were later summarised in his Apostolic Exhortation *Querida Amazonia* dated 2 February 2020.

This work argues that diplomacy, an art that has been central to the existence of the Vatican, became in the case of Pope Francis a way of life during his pontificate. Through his journeys abroad, starting with his visit to the Italian island of Lampedusa (2013) to his courageous visit to Iraq during pandemic and under security threats (2021), Pope Francis lived a call to peacemaking, and became a global player as a peacemaker. Thus, the publication of his encyclical on human fraternity *Fratelli Tutti* in Assisi on 3 October 2020 consolidated his role as a peacemaker with human fraternity as a central concern of his pontificate. Such idea, mandate, and role had already been outlined in his first appearance at St Peter's Square on the day of his election. His thought and global action regarding a human fraternity was emphasised by his signing of the document on Human Fraternity in Abu Dhabi in February 2019 that might be understood as a completion of his masterpiece on the common home for a fraternal and universal humanity, that is, his encyclical *Laudato Si'* (2015). Thus, throughout these years Pope Francis' ideas of human cooperation and a global human fraternity have been emphasised through his journeys outside the Vatican, and indeed outside Italy. Thus, Pope Francis' diplomacy from Rome reached the peripheries of this world. His journeys were personally chosen by him to foster diplomacy, peacekeeping, and dialogue within long-standing conflicts between and within nations, for example, Cuba and the United States, Burma and Bangladesh, the Central African Republic, Kenya, Iraq, and Colombia. Pope Francis' rationale and methodology was clear: to go personally to meet those involved and with gentleness help them to understand human and divine cooperation between countries, faith communities, and even spiteful enemies.

This work analyses some of Pope Francis' foreign journeys through primary sources, including all his speeches and meetings as a diplomat of peace. Among those visits this work outlines the most difficult ones, including his visits to Cuba and the United States before their agreement on diplomatic relations, and his meetings with Patriarch Bartholomew, patriarch of the Churches of the East, that ended an enmity between the East and West that went back to 1056, with a happy outcome: they became close friends, companions, and brothers on a journey of peacemaking. This work includes Pope Francis' mediation for peace in Colombia, Myanmar, and the Central African Republic where after years of civil war he brought together Christians and Muslims in Bangi. Within this work, the central themes considered are peacemaking, human fraternity, the common house, interreligious dialogue, and Pope Francis' contribution to a universal understanding of climate change and the environment, human migration, and a post-pandemic just social order.

Like other religious leaders such as the Dalai Lama, Pope Francis managed to exercise an international influence for peace that was directly linked to his movement towards others outside Europe and his journeys with them. Like Gandhi, Pope Francis rejected the idea of a diplomacy of compromises but has developed a sense of human beings, included himself, walking together in a common planet. Thus, two major statements have developed his life of diplomacy and efforts for peace within a common planet for Christians and Muslims, Buddhists, and Hindus, and all those who do not follow a religious path; see his encyclicals *Laudato Si'* (2015) and his statement of human fraternity *Fratelli Tutti* (October 2020). Pope Francis outlined a wide culture of universal fraternity and a clear commitment to a common house, that is, planet earth. Because of such writings, Pope Francis was voted as one of the most well-known individuals of the twenty-first century, precisely because in *Fratelli Tutti* he discussed his possible influence on a common peaceful international order after the global pandemic of COVID-19.

Contents of this volume

Chapter 1 explores the firm brotherhood and friendship of Pope Francis with Patriarch Bartholomew and the start of their common journey as peacemakers in Lampedusa (Italy), Cuba, and Abu Dhabi, and his difficult journeys to Muslims in Egypt and Turkey, to Jews and Muslims in Jordan and Jerusalem, and to Buddhists and Muslims in Sri Lanka, Myanmar, and Bangladesh. Most of those visits were made to states where violence and killings had taken place in the name of religion before his visits.

Chapter 2 explores the journeys and challenges undertaken by Pope Francis on his visits to Auschwitz and Hiroshima. On both occasions, Pope Francis spoke of human solidarity and peace within moments of extreme suffering. Following John XXIII's statement on peace and the end of nuclear weapons (*Pacem in Terris*, 1963), Pope Francis spoke of the possibilities of a real lasting peace in the contemporary world. In relation to his visit to Japan, it is extremely important to understand the wish of Pope Francis to visit Japan in the path of the first Jesuits and the Jesuits who helped the wounded in Japan after the use of the atomic bombs. Thus, the life of the Jesuit Pedro Arrupe and the challenge to extermination through force in Japan and Nazi Germany are central to such understanding because they became moments of silence, learning, and peacemaking for Pope Francis in the present. His sense of silence and his learning of history became powerful signs of his peacemaking.

Chapter 3 examines the role of Pope Francis as mediator in different contemporary circumstances through his own writings, letters, and Vatican documents. Pope Francis journeyed to help others in their efforts for peace, efforts that received a positive support by his arrival, including his visits to Colombia, Cuba and the United States, Myanmar and Bangladesh, and Kenya, Uganda, and the Central African Republic. Before the pandemic, he wanted to visit Syria and Iraq, but he was advised not to do so; however, in his visit during the pandemic Pope Francis influenced the peace efforts in Iraq in March 2021. Pope Francis' visit to the European Parliament followed such possibility of affecting peace by addressing European nations on their role of responsibility for peace. Pope Francis experienced the most difficult engagement of his pontificate in his visit to Chile, a previously prophetic Church, that stood accused of covering abuse in a large scale. As a result, Pope Francis welcomed victims to the Vatican and within an *ad limina* visit for all Chilean bishops he accepted their resignation leaving the Chilean Church as the only one in history to have had a full resignation of all bishops at the same time.

Chapter 4 examines Pope Francis' seminal writings on peace, social justice, and the common home, that is, *Laudato Si'* (2015) and *Fratelli Tutti* (2020). Pope Francis has shown how the life of

St Francis of Assisi has influenced him, and in turn Pope Francis has taken the actions by St Francis as central to his support for an ecological peace between those who destroy the planet and those who see themselves as stewards of creation. For Pope Francis, peace remains an issue closely linked to social justice and a just world economic order as well as the development of a fraternal universal humanity. Thus, following from the long-established social doctrine of the Church, for Pope Francis without justice and a just social order there is no peace.

Chapter 5 examines Pope Francis' encounter with world leaders, his visit to Iraq, and his engagement with migrants, refugees, and asylum seekers. Within the chapter Pope Francis' condemnation of selfishness and a lack of humanity in a post-pandemic climate bring his thought and action as a peacemaker into the future. For he is a peacemaker because he has the intention and the ability to bring humanity together. Such an agenda started in Lampedusa; it was reaffirmed through the Abu Dhabi Declaration, and it is brought into the future through *Fratelli Tutti*.

Pope Francis the peacemaker relies upon his previous pastoral ministry of peacemaking within Argentinean politics but brings a clear theoretical foundation to his actions of peace. Those important foundations are developed throughout this volume, being considered as fully complementary to his journeys, that is, synodality, subsidiarity, and collegiality. Thus, *synodality* as the outline of ecclesial decision-making remained for Pope Francis a place of dialogue in which decisions could be taken in common rather than imposed by him as Bishop of Rome; for example, Querida Amazonia (2020) comes out of the Amazonian Synod. *Subsidiarity* was the practice of such synodality by which the base could organise their own pastoral and daily communal life, as it was, for example, the case of the Amazonian Synod (6–27 October 2019). After the Synod, Pope Francis wrote Querida Amazonia, his apostolic exhortation, arguing for the plurality of the Church so that 'the history of the Church shows that Christianity does not have simply one cultural expression', and 'we would not do justice to the logic of the incarnation if we thought of Christianity as monocultural and monotonous'.[11] *Collegiality* refers to the plausibility of a body that having gone through dialogue within and with the world is able to stand together as a group that brings the firm sense of justice and peace to peacemaking efforts. Indeed, as this work would argue, as Pope Francis does.[12]

Notes

1 Pope Benedict XVI, 'Declaratio', from the Vatican 10 February 2013: 'After having repeatedly examined my conscience before God, I have come to the certainty that my strengths, due to an advanced age, are no longer suited to an adequate exercise of the Petrine ministry'.

2 Benedict XVI had dealt with the possibilities of a resignation in his 2010 interview with Peter Seewald; see Pope Emeritus Benedict XVI and Peter Seewald, *Light of the World: The Pope, the Church and the Signs of the Times*. San Francisco, CA: Ignatius Press, 2010.

3 *Laudato Si'* § 10.

4 These words spoken from the centre of Catholicism resounded to the ends of the world in the voice of Cardinal Jean-Louis Tauran: Annuntio vobis gaudium magnum: Habemus Papam! Eminentissimum ac Reverendissimum Dominum Georgium Marium Sanctae Romanae Ecclesiae Cardinalem Bergoglio qui sibi nomen imposiut Franciscum. Cardinal Bergoglio had chosen the name 'Francis', the saint of the poor.

5 For example, Pope Francis writing to the Heads of the Oriental Catholic Churches: 'Its is precisely being Bishop of Rome that is the foundation of the Petrine ministry, which is a service of presidency of charity and in charity (cf. Ign. Ant., *Letter to the Romans*, Proemio)', 'Address of His Holiness Pope Francis to the Patriarchs and Major Archbishops', *Bulletin of the Holy See Press office*, 9 October 2017.

6 Mario I. Aguilar, *Pope Francis: His Life and Thought*. Cambridge: The Lutterworth Press, 2014.

7 'Declaration of the Director of the Holy See Press Office, Matteo Bruni, 7 December 2020', *Summary of Bulletin Holy See Press Office*, 7 December 2020.

8 Pope Francis, 'Address of His Holiness Pope Francis to the Seventy-fifth Meeting of the General Assembly of the United Nations' 25 September 2020. Vatican City: Librería Editrice Vaticana, 2020.

9 Pope Francis, 'Address of His Holiness Pope Francis to the Seventy-fifth Meeting of the General Assembly of the United Nations' 25 September 2020. On the XIV Dalai Lama's sense of universal responsibility, see Mario I. Aguilar, *The 14th Dalai Lama:*

Peacekeeping and Universal Responsibility. London and New York: Routledge, 2021.

10 *Laudato Si'* § 13.

11 Pope Francis, *Querida Amazonía of the Holy Father Francis to the People of God and to all Persons of Good Will*, Post-Synodal Apostolic Exhortation, 2 February 2020 § 69.

12 See, for example, Pope Francis, Justin Welby (Archbishop of Canterbury), and Martin Fair (Moderator of the Church of Scotland), *Christmas Message to South Sudan Political Leaders*, Christmas 2020. Vatican City: Librería Editrice Vaticana.

1

AN INTERFAITH JOURNEY

When Pope Francis was elected as the Bishop of Rome in March 2013, he was following on the footsteps of two popes, John Paul II and Benedict XVI, who had been at the forefront of journeys outside the Vatican.[1] John Paul II particularly had experienced the centrality of Vatican mediations of peace between nations; for example, the end of the imminent war between Chile and Argentina in November/December 1978 due to disputed limits within the Beagle Strait.[2] John Paul II had been a hard act to follow and an example of a person who made many journeys meeting millions of people.[3] He was at ease with crowds while bored by Vatican Embassies' receptions. Benedict XVI travelled less but did so as a teacher, teaching doctrine and catholicity to those who listened to him.[4] Thus, when Pope Francis started his pontificate, it was assumed that at his age, he would not undertake many journeys outside Italy. However, once Pope Francis moved to the Vatican, he forcefully forwarded the agenda of the poor and the marginalised, of the common-home and ecological issues, and indeed started his pontificate with a clear sign: constant movement towards the Other was his central theological position. Pope Francis complemented his central position towards others in the peripheries by assuming Paul VI's ideas of progress and development in *Populorum Progressio* as his personal manifesto.[5] As a result of such manifesto, Pope Francis spoke of the plausibility of a contemporary better world in dialogue: *A better world will come about only if attention is first paid to individuals; if human promotion is integral, taking account of every*

*dimension of the person, including the spiritual; if no one is ne-
glected, including the poor, the sick, prisoners, the needy and the
stranger (cf. Mt 25:31–46); if we can prove capable of leaving
behind a throwaway culture and embracing one of encounter
and acceptance.*[6]

Papal journeys outside Italy became a common occurrence
since the time of Paul VI, who availing himself of the possibilities
of a developing air commercial transport, visited Colombia for
the Eucharistic Congress and the opening of the Second General
Meeting of Latin American Bishops in Medellin. On the same
year, 1968, Paul VI visited Uganda for the canonisation of the
Ugandan martyrs. Both journeys marked a new understanding
of the papacy as existing to affirm the life of Catholic communities outside Europe and to strengthen diplomatic ties between the
Vatican and countries that maintained diplomatic relations with
the Holy See. The Vatican State, founded in 1929 following the
signing of the Lateran Pacts between the Holy See and Italy on 11
February 1929, and ratified on 7 June 1929, is a functioning contemporary state with ministries and with ambassadors (Apostolic
Nuncios) throughout the world. John Paul II stressed the importance of papal visits to other states during his 25 years of pontificate. Pope Francis provided a continuity to such visits by choosing
to visit countries in which the Vatican had been particularly involved through processes of mediation, peace, and reconciliation,
as well as countries where a minority Catholic population needed
affirmation within interfaith dialogue. The visit to Cuba in 2015,
for example, strengthened new horizons of cooperation between
Cuba and the United States as well as providing the first working
meeting and mutual cooperation between a Pope and the Archbishop of Constantinople and Ecumenical Patriarch of the Orthodox Church (elected 1991), since the split of the Catholic Church
into East and West in 1056.[7] For example, in 2017 Pope Francis
decided to visit Myanmar with countless requests to go and find
out what was happening to the Rohingya. Before such visit, the
Pope had made ten apostolic visits outside Europe, with a visit to
Chile and Peru (January 2018) following his visit to Myanmar.[8]

A papal visit is a complex, challenging, and, inevitably, large-
scale event and requires intense preparation in advance because

there are many aspects to be looked at, including security, health, luggage, speeches, and even presents that need to be prepared and given by the Pope during his visits. The Pope and his delegation fly out of Italy in Alitalia, and he is usually transported from country to country by the national airline of the state he is visiting. Speeches that constitute the main preparation of a papal visit comprise a mixture of historical issues to be remembered and of new issues that are aired in public and usually discussed over a period after the papal visit. Thus, Pope Francis is aware that whatever he is going to say during a visit could mark diplomatic relations between the state he is visiting and the Vatican in the future. At the same time, the affirmation of Catholics and other faiths within a country is of the essence within a papal visit as well as the delivery of a clear public teaching on issues that could be contextually central to relations with the Vatican. Thus, in the case of the visit to Myanmar (2017), the eyes of the global media were set on the moment when Pope Francis addressed the government of Myanmar wondering if he was going to mention the Rohingya by name in public. He did not, and the media declared this a papal failure. Pope Francis decided not to mention the Rohingya, as he told journalists on his way back to the Vatican, as not to 'slam the door' on the face of his hosts. However, he was satisfied that in his private meeting with Aung San Suu Kyi and Myanmar's powerful military chief, General Min Aung Hlaing, he had been heard. Pope Francis had defined a papal visit during his first journey outside Europe, to Brazil, when he said that a papal visit was for the good of society, the good of young people, and the good of the elderly.

It is a fact that most countries in the world have diplomatic relations with the Holy See and that heads of state regularly visit the Vatican to discuss matters of common interest with the Pope. Thus, when the Pope decides to visit another state, it is for serious and pressing reasons. For example, Pope Francis' visit to the United States was a visit aimed at the affirmation of the Catholic communities after the scandals of child abuse, amid major discussions on the treatment of refugees, within ongoing racial and religious divisions, and after the opening of diplomatic conversations between the United States and Cuba. For the Pope cannot arrive in another country without the consent of the host government, and therefore common issues of interest are quickly established, and permissions granted either for a state visit, an apostolic visit, or a pastoral visit.

Journey to Lampedusa

Pope Francis' first papal visit was to Lampedusa, the island in southern Italy where so many boats sank, and migrants died, trying to reach the safety and protection of Italy and of the European Union.[9] Many of those migrants did not reach the point whereby according to the Dublin Protocol they needed to claim asylum at the first point of entry into the European Union. Pope Francis had reacted as many times he did with his own agenda rather than a present agenda, as he read reports on those migrants dying at sea. He could relate very closely to such experience of migration as his paternal grandparents had left Italy for Argentina with their six children looking for better opportunities. They had nearly died at sea as the ship they were initially booked in for the passage to Argentina, the Principessa Mafalda, sank.[10] There at Lampedusa, on the 8th of July 2013, Pope Francis prayed together with Patriarch Bartholomew for those who had lost their lives during the perilous journey, and greeted the many immigrants who attended the public Eucharist. The common humanity present at Lampedusa was not only human but also Christian as African immigrants started filling pews in parishes and churches, having sought employment caring for the elderly and filling jobs that had been avoided by young Italians.

For Pope Francis, and as outlined in the sixth anniversary of his visit to Lampedusa, 'migrants are the symbol of all those rejected by society'.[11] On the seventh anniversary of that memorable manifesto at the start of his pontificate Pope Francis, also confined by the pandemic in Rome, celebrated the Eucharist at Santa Marta together with health workers but making a clear point about the significance of such anniversary within a period of pandemic in the world. Furthermore, he remembered the conversations and narratives of prison and oppression the migrants had spoken of in Lampedusa.[12] In his homily, Pope Francis remembered his words concerning 'the globalization of indifference' when at Lampedusa he told those present that 'in this globalized world, we have fallen into globalized indifference. We have become used to the suffering of others: it doesn't affect me; it doesn't concern me; it's none of my business!'[13] However, in that search for a personal encounter with the Lord, 'the encounter with the other is also an encounter with Christ' for 'he is the one knocking in our door, hungry, thirsty, naked, sick, imprisoned; he is the one seeking an encounter with us, asking our help, asking to come ashore' (cf. Mt. 25:40).[14]

It could be argued that the interfaith journey and the deep friendship between Pope Francis and Patriarch Bartholomew started with such public display of concern for humanity in Lampedusa and continued during the seven years that followed. In every journey and every interaction with European leaders during those years after Lampedusa, Pope Francis stressed the demands of welcoming a suffering humanity to European shores during times in which suffering, war, and death surrounded such migrants' journeys. Welcoming them was not only an obligation under international law but an act of salvation welcoming them to the global Eucharistic celebration.[15] In 2013, Pope Francis, together with Patriarch Bartholomew, committed a wreath to the sea in memory of those who lost their lives at sea trying to make the crossing from Africa and the Middle East to Europe. In my African lectures at the Faculty of Theology of the University of Louvain, I opened such lectures with a reflection on the point of encounter between Africa and Europe. Africans are buried where they came from so that home is the place of a lineage, of ancestors, of a village that maybe many Africans have never lived in. The graveyards at the sea, made of thousands of migrants who attempted the crossing, unite Africa and Europe. The rescue boats of several European volunteer organisations are made of people who do not ask a political-border question about papers and rights, but they provide that hand of humanity in times of distress. The boats of migrants are not dissimilar of cargo boats of slaves who have entrusted their lives, in desperation of love for their families, to selfish human beings who manage to fill their boats with whoever wants to pay with disastrous consequences.

However, unlike the boats of slavery and the slave trade, this is our chance to free them and to welcome them because they are the Christ disembarking in Europe. The borders of Europe and the neat borders for immigration have become an impediment and a challenge not only to a universal humanity but also to a European-centred social doctrine of the Church.[16]

That exchange between the desperate poor, the carriers who profit by death, and the European states that receive them was deeply highlighted by Pope Francis' presence in the island of Lampedusa.[17] In the words of Tina Catania, Pope Francis made those immigrants visible within a Lampedusa that sits geographically at Italy's social margins.[18] Indeed, Pope Francis managed to unite the very Catholic sense of aiding migrants with discourses on religion in the field of international relations where religious and nonreligious actors respond to a humanitarian challenge.[19] It was the first journey away from Rome and a clear public sign of where the 'the boat of Peter' was going; it was not improvisation, but, according to Paulina Guzik, refugees and migrants constitute the core and trademark of Francis' pontificate.[20] The framework of synodality is clearly reflected in the first long journey towards others when Pope Francis recalls while celebrating the Eucharist with host Italians and migrants, God's question to Cain who had killed his brother: 'Cain, where is your brother?' For Pope Francis, 'the globalization of indifference has taken from us the ability to weep! In the Gospel we have heard the crying, the wailing, the great lamentation: "Rachel weeps for her children ... because they are no more"'.[21] And Pope Francis ends his address with the following powerful words: 'Today too, Lord, we hear you asking: "Adam, where are you?" "where is the blood of your brother?"'[22] The globalisation of indifference became the target for critiques against the markets and an economic system that was providing such framework of indifference being discussed by international articles on international finance.[23]

Against the globalisation of indifference

The opposite of indifference for Pope Francis was always dialogue, and particularly interfaith dialogue. Interfaith dialogue on the part of Francis is a coming-out of a dialogue within the globalisation of indifference. Thus, in interfaith dialogue and ecumenical dialogue it is possible to accept the status quo and to have good relations between religious groups. However, the consistent stand by Pope Francis was to try to do as much as possible as to bring together people of different faiths, to create conditions for peace and a common understanding. After Lampedusa it was possible to sense Pope Francis' personal concern regarding violence within the Central African Republic, a historical fact that triggered his visit to Bangui at the end of 2015. During that visit that came at the end of his visit to Kenya and Uganda, Pope Francis met with the Muslim community at the Central Mosque of Koudoukou, Bangui (30 November). In the mosque he addressed Muslims and referred to those who follow African indigenous (traditional) religions as follows: *Christians, Muslims and members of the traditional religions have lived together in peace for many years. They ought, therefore, to remain united in working for an end to every act which, from whatever side, disfigures the Face of God and whose ultimate aim is to defend particular interests by any and all means, to the detriment of the common good.*[24]

Pope Francis' constant ally and companion on his journeys was Patriarch Bartholomew I, 270th Archbishop of Constantinople and Ecumenical Patriarch since 2 November 1991, and spiritual leader of all Eastern Orthodox Christians worldwide. In November 2006, Patriarch Bartholomew had invited Pope Benedict XVI to visit him in Istanbul and to take part in the celebrations of St Andrew the Apostle, patron saint of the Church of Constantinople. At that time, Pope Benedict XVI recognised 'the momentous events that have sustained our commitment to work for the full unity of Catholics and Orthodox'.[25] Pope Benedict XVI stressed the seven Ecumenical Councils held in the East which Orthodox and Catholics 'acknowledge as authoritative for the faith and discipline of the Church'.[26] As a result of their meeting, theological dialogue was resumed.[27] In March 2013, Patriarch Bartholomew attended the inauguration of Pope Francis at the Vatican, the first papal inauguration attended by the Patriarch of Constantinople since the Great Schism between Eastern Churches and Rome in

1054. Indeed, in his foreword to *Primacy in the Church from Vatican I to Vatican II: An Orthodox Perspective*, Patriarch Bartholomew spoke of the issue of primacy as service of ministries and reaffirmed the practice of synodality as central to the Church's government and organisation.[28]

Relations between the Eastern Orthodox Church under Patriarch Bartholomew and Pope Francis leading Catholics of the Latin Rite and the Oriental Churches progressed very quickly not only because they wanted to stress what united them rather than the theological divisions concerning the Holy Spirit. Their approach was ecumenical and synodal in that they used their role of Primates of the West and of the East to find time for each other, journey together to different interfaith events, and finally celebrated St Andrews Day together in Constantinople. On that occasion, a deeply moved Pope Francis apologised for any harm done to the Eastern Orthodox in the name of religion. Such closeness was expressed during the Pandemic when Bartholomew supported several of Pope Francis' initiatives and his efforts to make peace with Muslims through the Declaration on Human Fraternity in Abu Dhabi (4 February 2019). Even within the 2020 pandemic, Pope Francis' delegates led by Cardinal Kurt Koch, President of the Pontifical Council for Promoting Christian Unity, greeted Patriarch Bartholomew in Istanbul.[29]

Pope Francis' visit to Turkey (28–30 November 2014) sealed their cooperation and friendship; a visit that included a meeting with the president, prime minister, and civil authorities of that country and a visit to the president of religious affairs (all at Ankara). In Istanbul, Pope Francis attended an Ecumenical Prayer in the Patriarchal Church of Saint George followed by a private meeting with H.H. Bartholomew I at the Patriarchal Palace. On the second day of his visit to Istanbul Pope Francis attended the Divine Liturgy in the Patriarchal Church of Saint George with an Ecumenical Blessing and the Signing of the Common Declaration. Pope Francis was deeply moved, and he embraced Bartholomew bowing to him while Bartholomew kissed Pope Francis' head. On that day Pope Francis also visited the Sultan Ahmet Mosque (Istanbul). At the mosque, the Pope did not join any other prayers by the Great Mufti, and they prayed standing side by side in their own traditions in silence. This was the custom brought by Pope Francis to all his visits to mosques and prayers with Muslims.

In Pope Francis' visit to Egypt (28–29 April 2017), there was a development in that a logo and a motto were used: 'Pope of Peace in Egypt of Peace'. Furthermore, a personal video message was delivered by Pope Frances in Rome before the visit. The visit was a state visit in that Pope Francis met with the President of the Republic and had a state welcoming ceremony. However, the main invitation had come from the Grand Imam of Al-Azhar to participate in an International Peace Conference. In his speech at the conference, Pope Francis stressed the birth and contribution of the Egyptian civilisation and gave less importance to the past divisions with Islam. Later, Pope Francis paid a courtesy visit to H.H. Pope Tawadros II, and a common declaration was signed between the Coptic Orthodox Patriarchate of Egypt and the Catholic Church with one purpose: an agreement that established not to repeat the baptism administered in the Coptic Orthodox Church or the Catholic Church when one person decided to change from one community to the other. During his visit, Pope Francis visited Al-Azhar headquarters in Cairo where he also prayed in silence together with the Grand Imam of Al-Azhar, Ahmed el-Tayeb.

It could be argued that Pope Francis followed the example of dialogue with and understanding of Islam previously mediated by Cardinal Jean-Louis Tauran, a French cardinal who was previously the proto-deacon (2011–2014) and President of the Pontifical Council for Interreligious Dialogue (2014–2019). As Camerlengo, Tauran announced Bergoglio's election as Pope Francis. Cardinal Tauran was very close to Muslims, and he drove a full agenda of interreligious dialogue with the Islamic World. He had been a French soldier in Algeria and later he had the experience of the followers of Charles de Foucauld of prayer in the desert. As part of his agenda, he attended the annual gathering of different religious leaders in Muscat, Oman, and became a fearful proposer of a dialogue between Israel and Palestine with a two-state solution as policy by the Vatican. Thus, Pope Francis' first state visit was to Israel mediated by Tauran's close ally, the

King of Jordan. Tauran had been influenced by his meetings with and reading of the writings of moderate Islamic intellectuals such as Shaikh Abdullah bin Mohammed al Salmi (Oman) and Sayyid Mohammad Khatami (Iran). Al Salmi was the main instigator of the interreligious international agenda by Sultan Qaboos bin Said of Oman, and Khatami responded forcefully to any theory of a clash of civilisations with his own 'dialogue of civilisations'.

In a retrospective look at history, the contribution of Al Salmi and Khatami can be related to Pope Francis' encounter with the Grand Imam of Al-Azhar Ahmed el-Tayeb and the signing of the document on 'Human Fraternity for World Peace and Living Together' on 4 February 2019. During 2019, the United Arab Emirates declared the 'Year of Tolerance' and welcomed the Grand Imam of Al-Azhar and Pope Francis to Abu Dhabi. On the same 4th February 2019, Pope Francis addressed an interreligious meeting at the Founder's Memorial in Abu Dhabi where he remembered the eighth centenary of the meeting of Saint Francis of Assisi and Sultan al-Malik al-Kamil; on that occasion, Pope Francis declared that he had come 'as a believer thirsting for peace, as a brother seeking peace with the brethren'.[30] However, Pope Francis reminded those present that 'the enemy of fraternity is an individualism which translates into the desire to affirm oneself and one's own group above others'. Furthermore, Pope Francis spoke about the requirement of human fraternity and of 'the duty to reject every nuance of approval from the word "war"'.[31]

The meeting between Pope Francis and the Grand Imam of Al-Azhar has remained a central pillar of our understanding of a shared humanity in which 'faith leads a believer to see in the other a brother or sister to be supported and loved'.[32] After the interfaith dialogue meeting, they signed the document on *Human Fraternity*. From the start of the document they made clear that such human fraternity needs a public rather than a private expression and that such expression finds a purpose in 'safeguarding creation and the entire universe and supporting all persons, especially the poorest and those most in need'.[33] Both religious leaders provided a liberating praxis by acting on their leadership through reflections on issues that affect a common humanity, and certainly Muslims and Christians; for example, poverty, conflict, and suffering in different parts of the world. They also isolated issues that could be considered 'structural sins' and that are causes of poverty and suffering: the arms race, social injustice, corruption, inequality, moral decline, terrorism, discrimination, and extremism.[34] A document on *Human Fraternity* came out of such encounter 'as a guide for future generations to advance a culture of mutual respect in the awareness of the great divine grace that makes all human beings brothers and sisters'.[35]

The text of *Human Fraternity* opens a series of inclusive categories with the expression 'In the name of' following the opening of the Koran so that the first opening in the text reads as follows: 'In the name of God who has created all human beings equal in rights, duties and dignity, and who has called them to live together as brothers and sisters, to fill the earth and make known the values of goodness, love, and peace'.[36] Thus, the document becomes a joint declaration of good and heartfelt aspirations in the name of God, innocent human life, the poor, the destitute, the marginalised, orphans, widows, refugees, and those exiled from their homes and their countries, people who have lost their security, peace, and the possibility of living together, human fraternity, fraternity torn apart by policies of extremism and division, freedom, justice, and mercy, and all persons of good will present in every part of the world. The adherence to the document not only was an unexpected path of understanding but included Al-Azhar al-Sharif and the Muslims of East and West as well as the Catholic Church and the Catholics of East and West. They together declared 'the adoption of a culture of dialogue as the path; mutual cooperation as the code of conduct; reciprocal understanding as the method and standard'. They condemned practices that are not part of religions as expressions of the belief in God, including genocide, acts of terrorism, forced displacement, human organ trafficking, abortion, and euthanasia. The conclusions of *Human Fraternity* express their aspiration that 'this Declaration may constitute an invitation to reconciliation and fraternity among all believers, indeed among believers and non-believers, and among all people of God will'.

In summary, the visits by Pope Francis to Turkey and Egypt were seminal to the plausibility of a religious unity in diversity. Religion is a complex phenomenon that humanly brings the possibility of 'the dialogue of civilisations', 'the dialogue of a shared humanity', and the enormous plausibility of a 'human fraternity'. Thus, such documents express a human desire to serve the divine unity and to reflect on the possibilities of a human journey of faith. Pope Francis argued that in order to engage in dialogue, one party or the other must leave their comfort, and journey just as the founders Mohamed and Jesus did, by going to others. They must look for opportunities to share understandings and to encounter differences, not with the sadness of the incomplete understanding but with the plausibility of the common journey. Thus, Pope Francis' journeys have brought other partners into the conversation: pilgrims such as Patriarch Bartholomew and the Muslims of Egypt and the United Arab Emirates.

In Pope Francis' peacekeeping efforts, the complexity of dialogue assumed that the formality of a theological diplomacy incorporates the contextual action of dialogue between different civilisations. As a result, the 'dialogue of civilisations' becomes the competition for God's love in which different manners of approach and of interconnectedness are negotiated. With Cardinal Tauran as an example, the diplomacy of listening and encountering without an immediate response or solution assumes an ongoing possibility of friendship and the sitting together of members of a common family. Indeed, the contemporary Christian–Muslim dialogue has been the most challenging but the most transcendent of Pope Francis' papacy. The warmth of unknown partners has become an ongoing visit to friends, and the friends have brought their families with them as it was the case of the papal visit to Jordan where the king's family waited for Pope Francis at their living room to share some tea and some sweets, including the king's children. And indeed, Pope Francis has brought his mere humanity and warmth to this dialogue and possible partners have responded. Diplomacy has become the centre of encounter so that very recently Pope Francis has indicated that all future trainees at the Vatican academy must spent a year in a context of service with the very poor of this world.

I would argue that such journey will continue, and I would like to end this reflection on interfaith dialogue as liberating praxis with the words of my mentor the late Cardinal Tauran: 'After the "dialogue with the world" of Paul VI, the "dialogue of peace" of John Paul II, the "dialogue of love and truth" of Benedict XVI, we have come to the challenge of interreligious dialogue as "dialogue of friendship", announced by Pope Francis'.[37]

Through Tauran, such dialogue was expanded through the diplomatic efforts by Tauran as Vatican Secretary for Relations with States. Those efforts provided a link between the sociopolitical action of liberation theology and the praxis of the encounter with other religions that were to become central in the agenda of the twenty-first century and the pandemic and the post-pandemic phases. One of those efforts was the cooperation between the different religions in combating human trafficking. In 2002, Tauran presided the international conference 'Twenty-First Century Slavery – The Human Rights Dimension to Trafficking in Human Beings'. For that conference Pope John Paul II wrote a letter outlining his own close interest on this example of structural sin and outlined some of the important matters that were going to be discussed during the conference. The problem and sin of human trafficking became an example of the practical connections between faith communities in dialogue that started by acting on its denunciation through the liberating praxis of action to eliminate human trafficking, a concern that became part of Pope Francis' agenda later.

Notes

1 See for example, James Ramon Felak, *The Pope in Poland: The Pilgrimages of John Paul II 1979–1991*. Pittsburgh, PA: University of Pittsburgh Press, 2021, and Peter Seewald, *Benedict XVI: An Intimate Portrait*. San Francisco, CA: Ignatius Press, 2008.

2 Pope John Paul II, 'Audiencia del Santo Padre Juan Pablo II a las delegaciones de Argentina y Chile', 23 April 1982. Vatican City: Librería Editrice Vaticana.

3 For example, if one takes 1986 as an example, he visited India (1–10 February), Prato, Italy (19 March), Romagna (8–11 May), Colombia and St Lucia (1–8 July), Aosta Valley (6–7 September), France (4–7 October), Fiesole and Florence (18–19 October), Perugia and

Assisi (26–27 October), and Bangladesh, Singapore, Fiji, New Zealand, Australia, and Seychelles (19 November–1 December).

4 For example, during 2008, Benedict XVI had only three journeys outside Italy with clear purposes rather than national visits, that is, the United States and the United Nations (15–21 April), Sydney, Australia on the 23rd World Youth Day, and his visit to Lourdes on the 150th anniversary of the apparition of the Blessed Virgin Mary at Lourdes (12–15 September).

5 Paul VI, *Populorum Progressio, Encyclical of Pope Paul VI on the Development of Peoples.* Vatican City: Librería Editrice Vaticana, 26 March 1967.

6 Pope Francis, 'Message of his holiness Pope Francis for the world day of migrants and refugees (2014), "Migrants and refugees: Towards a better world"', 5 August 2013. Vatican City: Librería Editrice Vaticana.

7 Since 2015 Pope Francis and Patriarch Bartholomew have gone together to pray in Lampedusa and have attended together the 500th anniversary of the Protestant Reformation in Sweden (2016). They both share a theological interest on ecological issues; see Pope Francis, *Carta Encíclica Laudato Si' del Santo Padre Francisco sobre el cuidado de la casa común.* Santiago: SAN PABLO y Paulinas, 2015, who cites Patriarch Bartholomew, 'Discurso en Santa Bárbara', California 8 November 1977, in *Laudato Si'* §8–9, and John Chryssavgis, *On Earth as in Heaven: Ecological Vision and Initiatives of Ecumenical Patriarch Bartholomew.* New York: Bronx, 2012.

8 Brazil (July 2013); Holy Land and Jordan (May 2014); Korea (August 2014); Turkey (November 2014); Sri Lanka and the Philippines (January 2015); Ecuador, Bolivia, and Paraguay (July 2015); Cuba, the United States, and the United Nations in New York (September 2015); Kenya, Uganda, and the Central African Republic (November 2015); Mexico (February 2016); Egypt (April 2017); and Colombia (September 2017).

9 According to Fortress Europe, approximately 6,450 people died in the Channel of Sicily between 1994 and 2012; see 'Pope Francis visits migrant island to lament "Globalisation of Indifference"', *International Business Times*, 8 July 2013.

10 Christopher Lamb, *The Outsider: Pope Francis and His Battle to Reform the Church.* Maryknoll, NY: Orbis, 2020, p. 47.

11 Pope Francis, 'Migrants are the symbol of all those rejected by society: Pope Francis' mass on the sixth anniversary of his visit to Lampedusa', *L'Osservatore Romano* 12 July 2019, p. 12.

12 Pope Francis, 'Fleeing the hell of detention camps: On the seventh anniversary of his visit to Lampedusa, the Pope recalls the experiences of the migrants he met there', *L'Osservatore Romano*, 10 July 2020, p. 3.

13 Pope Francis, Visit to Lampedusa, 'Homily of Holy Father Francis', 'Arena' sports camp, Salina Quarter, Monday, 8 July 2013. Vatican City: Librería Editrice Vaticana, 2013.

14 Pope Francis, Eucharistic celebration to open the meeting of reception structures, 'Liberi dalla paura' ('Free from fear'), Fraterna Domus of Sacrofano (Rome) 15 February 2019.

15 Daniel G. Groody, 'Cup of suffering, chalice of salvation: Refugees, Lampedusa, and the Eucharist', *Theological Studies* 78/4, December 2017, pp. 960–987.

16 Anna Rowlands, 'After Lesvos and Lampedusa: The European "crisis" and its challenge to Catholic social thought', *Journal of Catholic Social Thought* 14/1, 2017, pp. 63–85.

17 Carmen Lora, 'Dramas de la migración', *Páginas* 44/255, September 2019, pp. 86–92.

18 Tina R. Catania, 'Making immigrants visible in Lampedusa: Pope Francis, migration, and the state', *Italian Studies* 70/4, November 2015, pp. 465–486.

19 John A. Rees and Stephania Rawson, 'The resources of religious humanitarianism: The case of migrants on Lampedusa', *Journal for the Academic Study of Religion* 31/2, 2018, pp. 172–191.

20 Paulina Guzik, 'Communicating migration: Pope Francis' strategy of reframing refugee issues', *Church, Communication and Culture* 3/2, May 2018, pp. 106–135.

21 Pope Francis, 'Visit to Lampedusa: Homily of Holy Father Francis'.

22 See also Alessandro Gisotti, 'Where is your brother?', *L'Osservatore Romano*, 10 July 2020, pp. 1, 6.

23 For example, see 'Pope Francis visits migrant island to lament "Globalisation of Indifference"', *International Business Times*, 8 July 2013.

24 Apostolic Journey of His Holiness Pope Francis to Kenya, Uganda, and the Central African Republic (25–30 November 2015), Meeting with the Muslim Community, 'Address of His Holiness Pope Francis', Central Mosque of Koudoukou, Bangui (Central African Republic), Monday, 30 November 2015. Vatican City: Librería Editrice Vaticana.

25 Pope Benedict XVI, Apostolic Journey of His Holiness Benedict XVI to Turkey (28 November–1 December 2006), Meeting with His Holiness Bartholomew I Ecumenical Patriarch of Constantinople, 'Address of the Holy Father', Patriarchal Cathedral of Saint George in the Phanar, Istanbul, Wednesday, 29 November 2006. Vatican City: Librería Editrice Vaticana.

26 Pope Benedict XVI, 'Address of the Holy Father', Patriarchal Cathedral of Saint George in the Phanar, Istanbul, Wednesday, 29 November 2006.

27 Benedictus PP. XVI and Bartholomew I, 'Common Declaration of Pope Benedict XVI and the Ecumenical Patriarch Bartholomew I', from the Phanar, 30 November 2006. Vatican City: Librería Editrice Vaticana.

28 His All-Holiness Ecumenical Patriarch Bartholomew, 'Foreword', in Maximos Vgenopoulos, *Primacy in the Church from Vatican I to Vatican II: An Orthodox Perspective*. DeKalb: Northern Illinois University Press, 2013.

29 Message of the Holy Father to Ecumenical Patriarch for the Feast of Saint Andrew: The primary duty of dialogue.

30 Apostolic Journey of His Holiness Pope Francis to the United Arab Emirates, 3–5 February 2019, Interreligious Meeting, Address of His Holiness, Founder's Memorial (Abu Dhabi), Monday 4 February 2019, Vatican City: Librería Editrice Vaticana.

31 Pope Francis cited from the Interreligious General Audience on the Occasion of the 50th Anniversary of the Promulgation of the Conciliar Declaration 'Nostra Aetate', St Peter's Square, Wednesday 28 October 2015, Vatican City: Librería Editrice Vaticana, cf. Nostra Aetate § 5.

32 'Introduction' to *A Document on Human Fraternity for World Peace and Living Together*, Abu Dhabi, 4 February 2019, Vatican City: Librería Editrice Vaticana.

33 'Introduction' to *A Document on Human Fraternity for World Peace and Living Together*.

34 'Introduction' to *A Document on Human Fraternity for World Peace and Living Together*.

35 'Introduction' to *A Document on Human Fraternity for World Peace and Living Together*.

36 *A Document on Human Fraternity for World Peace and Living Together*.

37 '50th anniversary celebration of the Pontifical Council for Interreligious Dialogue: Welcome of Cardinal Jean-Louis Tauran', 19 May 2014, The Vatican; https://www.pcinterreligious.org/jeanlouis-tauran-en-2014

2

FROM AUSCHWITZ TO
HIROSHIMA

The previous chapter explored the development of ecumenism between the Catholic Church and the Orthodox Churches under Pope Francis, and the healing of wounds that went back a long way to the Schism of 1054 and the pillage by the Christian Crusaders of Constantinople during the Crusades.[1] The closeness of Pope Francis and Patriarch Bartholomew and their visit to Lampedusa marked the beginning of Pope Francis' papacy as one of dialogue against the globalisation of indifference, and a papacy in which dialogue between religions was central to the creation of the conditions for a global peace. Such encounters between Christian leaders were extended to Muslims through visits to Egypt and Turkey as well as through the signing of the Declaration of Human Fraternity in Abu Dhabi. This chapter explores journeys of peacemaking as healing by Pope Francis. Within such journeys, and particularly his journeys to places of mass killings and human atrocities in the context of war, Pope Francis emphasised the foundational peace of nations not only as the absence of war but as the presence of dialogue and as common human journeys. Within these visits, first to the former concentration camp of Auschwitz and later to Hiroshima and Nagasaki, Pope Francis used silence and solidarity as the key to a peaceful future. Within such visits he carried with him the absolute conviction of previous popes, starting with John XXIII, that war was not an option and that nuclear weapons were not to be used as arms of

DOI: 10.4324/9781003172345-3

deterrence. John XXIII had written in his encyclical *Pacem in Terris* (1963):

> Hence justice, right reason, and the recognition of man's dignity cry out insistently for a cessation to the arms race. The stockpile of armaments which have been built in various countries must be reduced and round and simultaneously by the parties concerned. Nuclear weapons must be banned.[2]

Proclaiming peace in Auschwitz

On Friday 29 July 2016 Pope Francis visited Auschwitz-Birkenau in the context of his visit to Poland.[3] John Paul II and Benedict XVI also visited the extermination camps during their pontificates. Indeed, John Paul II visited Auschwitz several times before becoming Pope in order to pray at the cell where St Maximilian Kolbe had died.[4] Benedict XVI accompanied John Paul II on that day in June 1979 as archbishop of Munich-Freising and later visited Auschwitz as Pope, being aware that he visited as 'a son of the German people'.[5] A man of reason, Benedict XVI spoke of God in the following terms: 'The God in whom be believe is a God of reason – a reason, to be sure, which is not a kind of cold mathematics of the universe, but is one with love and with goodness'.[6] Pope Francis' visit was somehow different because silence was his practice during the visit. His visit reminded me of my own memories of captivity at the Villa Grimaldi (Chile) which I have outlined elsewhere and my first return to the torture camp in silence.[7] The silence that Pope Francis brought to the memory of the Shoah was highlighted by his pursuit of two eremitic actions: he sat silently at the entrance of Auschwitz on a chair for what it seemed an endless time and later he sat in darkness and in silence in the cell where Maximilian Kolbe (1894–1941), a priest who gave his life for another human being, was kept before his execution.[8] It seems that death and silence go always together, and death remains a moment of profound definition for the rest of humanity, particularly in unjust and cruel circumstances.[9]

Such silent recognition of the suffering of many, most of them Jews, and who died in Auschwitz, was a public recognition by Pope Francis of the common journey that all followers of the world religions can pursue together. Such common journey by all religious communities and all human beings at one point or another have been violently marked by disruption, violent attacks, and killings. They share a history, and they share a journey if they decide to accept this human commonality. It is within such silence that peace and understanding in a common journey can challenge any message of hatred and violence towards others. Indeed, Pope Francis' journeys to Auschwitz and Japan were silent visits in which he stood in silence in solidarity with historical suffering and with the spoils and monuments to the dead that reminded him of national ideologies and war. We must remember that Pope Francis had the experience of human rights abuses by the military in Argentina and of bombings in his own country against members of the Jewish community of Buenos Aires. Pope Francis' silence was also poignant when he addressed the world from St Peter's Square in March 2020, in the middle of the COVID-19 pandemic. As it happened in Auschwitz and Hiroshima his frail figure stood in silence leading a suffering humanity and asking God for peace within his own search for peace between churches, communities, and nations.

The hermeneutics of silence

The interpretation of silence as a moment in time and space reminds us that silence is a creative moment for the self and for the context in which such silence takes place. It is not only the physical silence that can be created but the silence of the soul, the silence of the heart, and ultimately the silence of the self. The interpretation of such silent movement recreates three spheres of understanding that provide in turn three layers in which silence becomes the link between the first level of the individual self, the second level of a personal transformation, and the third level of existence within a cosmic world. It is in that cosmic world beyond humanity in which silence reigns that silence becomes a song, a rainbow, a cosmic canticle. If silence can be interpreted as the creative and meaningful link between the first and the third levels, death becomes within the second level the means to an end, the maturation of the self to enter the cosmic realm of existence. Thus, to interpret silence in all its creativity and to experience such silence requires the silencing of the word to focus on what comes before the word, which is silence.[10] For Raimon Panikkar, for example, the expression 'In the beginning was the Word' is not a claim that the Word is the beginning. Rather, 'the Beginning is Silence, the Void, Non-Being, the Abyss, Darkness, or other symbols in many other traditions'.[11] The Word is not silent, and it is not silence, Panikkar argues, but 'the true word emerges from the silence, "shattering" it, going beyond it, overcoming it' so that 'silence doesn't speak, it says nothing, but it makes the saying possible; Silence inspires it, since it dwells there'.[12] It is in silence that reality is united because 'silence is one, words are many'.[13]

It is this possibility of silence as a creative communal moment before the word is spoken that Pope Francis emphasised in his conscious wish not to speak at Auschwitz but to remain silent. He had expressed such wish in the following words: 'I would like to go to that place of horror without speeches, without crowds – only the few people necessary', he explained. 'Alone, enter, pray. And may the Lord give me the grace to cry'.[14] *Memoria e silenzio* (memory and silence) were the headlines of *L'Osservatore Romano*, the daily Vatican newspaper in the edition that reported the visit one day later.[15]

The hermeneutics of death

It was through moments of silence, extended ones for any previous papal visit, that Francis tried to comprehend death at Auschwitz.[16] He arrived by car at the entrance to the museum and then walked on his own through the main gates, slowly into the camp, as many prisoners had done during those years in which 1.1 million people were exterminated, most of them Jews. The camp had been built around the city of Oswiecim and established in 1940 as Polish citizens taken as prisoners after the Nazi invasion of Poland increased in numbers.[17] Once inside the camp he sat on a chair located at Roll Call Square for a period reflecting and praying, trying not to be disturbed by the Vatican photographer or the security that kept a watchful eye on those passing by. At the end of this period in silence Pope Francis kissed one of the wooden pillars and departed for the wall on which prisoners were executed, a wall destroyed by the camp guards (1943) and rebuild by prisoners later (1946). Another long moment of silence took place at the cell where Fr Maximilian Kolbe had died, now a publicly proclaimed saint for the Catholic Church. The cell is in the underground of block 11 and the cell is number 18. The cell has a plaque and a candle donated by Pope John Paul II.

Fr Kolbe had made the ultimate sacrifice willingly at a time when a Polish man was going to be sent to the block where prisoners were starved to death. It was the order of the commandant of Auschwitz that for every escapee ten prisoners were to be sent to the starvation block where they died of hunger and thirst. In one of those occasions and when ten prisoners had been chosen a Polish man cried wondering what would happen to his wife and children. Fr Kolbe stepped forward, identified himself as a Catholic priest to the camp commander, and asked that he be sent to the starvation block instead of the man who cried. Kolbe argued that he did not have a family and that the man had a family to return to. The commander agreed to the request and Kolbe was sent to the starvation block where two weeks later he was given a lethal injection as he was one of the last prisoners left to die. His body was burnt together with many other bodies.

Pope Francis remained in silence within the dark cell and later signed the book of honour with the words, 'Lord, have mercy on your people, Lord, forgiveness for so much cruelty' (Franciscus 29.7.2016). The silence of such poignant moments was then changed for an emotional meeting with some of the camp survivors who showed him photos and whom he embraced. And he departed for Birkenau, an extension of the Auschwitz camp.

Meeting with the righteous ones

Pope Francis visited and prayed at the Monument to the Victim of the Nations, inaugurated in 1967 between Crematoria II and

III. There is a phrase written on the tombstones in 23 languages spoken by prisoners: 'For ever let this place be a cry of despair and a warning to humanity, where the Nazis murdered about one and a half million men, women and children, mainly Jews, from various countries of Europe. Auschwitz-Birkenau 1940–1945'. Pope Francis prayed in silence and lit a candle with a 1,000 people in attendance. He met 25 'Righteous among the Nations', that is non-Jews who saved Jews from Nazi persecution. After that meeting a Rabbi recited Psalm 130 in Hebrew, text that was read in Polish by one of the survivors.

The presence of the 'Righteous' provided the possibility of a reflection on the availability of goodness and a common journey. For during any horror there are choices, and some of those choices are to aid even those who are not one's kin or one's people. Thus, in the preface to the diary of Carl Schrade, a Swiss national who spent 11 years in different Nazi concentration camps, Fabrice d'Almeida argues that 'regardless of circumstances or duties there is always the possibility of behaving as a human being and of preserving the highest sentiments of human nature' [my translation].[18] Yad Vashem, the World Holocaust Remembrance Center, outlines the 'Righteous' as follows: 'They were ordinary human beings, and it is precisely their humanity that touches us and should serve as a model. So far Yad Vashem has recognized "Righteous" from 44 countries and nationalities; there are Christians from all denominations and churches, Muslims and agnostics; men and women of all ages; they come from all walks of life; highly educated people as well as illiterate peasants; public figures as well as people from society's margins; city dwellers and farmers from the remotest corners of Europe; university professors, teachers, physicians, clergy, nuns, diplomats, simple workers, servants, resistance fighters, policemen, peasants, fishermen, a zoo director, a circus owner, and many more'.[19] It is the possibility of acting ethically regardless of being caught and in danger of death that makes a human being honest and good. The silence of complicity has been invoked for too long as the only possible response in time of mass killings. However, those honest and ethical responses to a very serious historical period come out of a life of small responses by witnesses to suffering and of a personal prayer that brings the response to the Gospel and to life as clearly opposed to the silence of complicity in the face of death. Today, and in our contemporary context, I could think that when homosexuals or transsexuals have been killed in homophobic attacks all of us who did not challenge somebody who made a small homophobic remark are accomplices of such death. Jokes and remarks against Jews today certainly prepare a violent act that can be stopped when the initial remark has been uttered in a bar, or in a dinner, or in a corridor.

It is the possibility of silence that allows us to know about those who died, particularly those who died at the Shoah for being ethnically Jewish and whose descendants live among us today. The ethical responsibility of not forgetting them is not only a Jewish duty but also a Christian duty: to remember all those human beings who died unjustly under machineries of extermination and hate. We are all human beings on a journey, and the silence of Pope Francis allowed for a very public sign that spoke to us about the meaningful silence of a suffering common humanity. The visit to Auschwitz preceded a very similar mode of visiting but far away: Hiroshima and Nagasaki.

Hiroshima and Nagasaki

Pope Francis visited Thailand and Japan in November 2019 (19–26). As a Jesuit, he was mindful of the Jesuit missionaries sent by Ignatius of Loyola to Asia, and particularly those who arrived in Japan. As a young Jesuit he found inspiration in the martyrs of Japan as other Argentinean Jesuits did and who were sent to Japan by him, at that time Father Jorge Mario Bergoglio, provincial of the Argentinean Jesuits.[20] However, his visit to Japan in 2019 was preceded by his arrival in Thailand where, escorted by his cousin who was a religious sister in Thailand and who became his official interpreter, he greeted King Maha Vajiralongkorn 'Rama X' at Amphorn Royal Palace. Pope Francis visited religious dignitaries such as the Supreme Buddhist Patriarch at Wat Ratchabophit Sathit Maha Simaram Temple and had a meeting with leaders, other Christian traditions, and religions.

On 18 November 2019, he delivered a video message to those awaiting his visit to Japan.[21] Pope Francis spoke about his words of friendship to Japan remembering the visit's motto 'Protect All Life'. The dignity of human life, according to Pope Francis, needs to be protected during threats by armed conflicts. And further, he prayed that the destructive power of nuclear weapons be never used again, for 'using nuclear weapons is immoral'. Pope Francis also spoke about the importance of the culture of dialogue, of fraternity between the different religious traditions that creates the possibility of a peace that is secure, and it lasts.[22]

Pope Francis departed for Tokyo from Bangkok and arrived at Tokyo-Haneda Airport on Saturday 23 November 2019. He met with the Japanese bishops at the Apostolic Nunciature and on the following day departed for Nagasaki. At 10.15 a.m., Pope Francis delivered his main speech on nuclear weapons at the Atomic Bomb Hypocenter Park.[23] In a very rainy day, he delivered one of the main policymaking texts of his pontificate to a Japanese audience and in Spanish. Pope Francis first recalled the importance of Nagasaki as a reminder of the pain and horror that human beings can inflict on each other, and he recalled the recently found part of the Nagasaki cathedral cross and the statue of Our Lady, reminders of those who suffered due to the bomb. He mentioned security, peace, and stability as desired human values, but he quickly added that 'the possession of nuclear and other weapons of mass destruction is not the answer to this desire'. For 'peace and international stability are incompatible with attempts to build upon the fear of mutual destruction or the threat of total annihilation'. Instead, peace and international stability can only be achieved through a global ethics of solidarity and cooperation. Thus, for Pope Francis, 'a world of peace, free from nuclear weapons, is the aspiration of millions of men and women anywhere'.[24] He spoke about 'an erosion of multilateralism' and the efforts needed not only by individuals but also organisations, states, and international bodies to stop the arms race and to work together towards dialogue and cooperation. The Catholic Church, according to Pope Francis, is committed to peace at global level. Thus, as a sign of that commitment to peace the Japanese bishops in July 2018 launched an appeal for the abolition of nuclear weapons, and each August the Catholic Church in Japan holds a ten-day prayer meeting for peace. His public statement was very clear: 'Convinced as I am that a world without nuclear weapons is possible and necessary, I ask political leaders not to forget that these weapons cannot protect us from current threats to national and international security'. For Pope Francis, the current situation on nuclear weapons needed to be reviewed considering the complex implementation of the 2030 Agenda for Sustainable Development, as to achieve an integrated human development.[25] Finally, he concluded that 'No one can turn a blind eye to the ruin caused by a culture incapable of dialogue' and invited those present, Catholics and non-Catholics, to pray to St Francis of Assisi prayer for peace.

On the same day, Pope Francis flew to Hiroshima and took part in a Meeting for Peace at the Hiroshima Peace Memorial.[26] There he wrote a message to mark the occasion, laid a flower offering, and listened to the atomic bomb survivors' testimonies. It was a moment of silence because survivors spoke in Japanese without immediate translation, and Pope Francis aided by an Argentinean Jesuit spoke to each of them one by one in Spanish. It was dark and evening time, and Pope Francis delivered his speech in Spanish. Pope Francis recalled that in Hiroshima in an instant many dreams and hopes disappeared 'leaving behind only shadows and silence'. What was left was a black hole of destruction and death so that 'from that abyss of silence, we continue even today to hear the cries of those who are no longer with us'. Pope Francis continued paying homage to the survivors as a 'pilgrim of peace' saying, 'Here I pay homage to all the victims, and I bow before the strength and dignity of those who, having survived those first moments, for years afterward bore in the flesh immense suffering, and in their spirit seeds of death that drained their vital energy'. Pope Francis wanted to visit Hiroshima to stand in silent prayer in a place of memory and hope for the future bringing the cry of the poor, being the voice of the voiceless who always are the ones who pay for the lack of care for the common home and for armed conflicts.

During his speech Pope Francis rejected the very existence of nuclear weapons stating

> with deep conviction I wish once more to declare that the use of atomic energy for purposes of war is today, more than ever, a crime not only against the dignity of human beings but against any possible future for our common home. The use of atomic energy for purposes of war is immoral, just as the possessing of nuclear weapons is immoral.

Thus, following John XXIII, Pope Francis stated clearly that peace is no more than an empty word if it is not 'founded on truth, built up in justice, animated and perfected by charity, and attained in freedom'.[27] For 'no one can love with offensive weapons in their hands'.[28] For Pope Francis following the tradition of the Catholic Church affirmed once again that 'peace is not merely the absence of war'.[29] Instead, he argued in Hiroshima that 'peace is the fruit of justice, development, solidarity, care for our common home and the promotion of the common good, as we have learned from the lessons of history'. Pope Francis was clear in Hiroshima that war was not a situation that could be welcome and that we are all united not only by the interconnectedness of globalisation but also by a common earth in which we all live together. His final prayer was loud and immediate: 'Come, Lord, for it is late, and where destruction has abounded, may hope also abound today that we can write and achieve a different future. Come, Lord, Prince of Peace! Make us instruments and reflections of your peace!'

Pope Francis had fulfilled his dream to visit Japan, and the peacemaker was intent on continuing his foreign visits to bring people together and create a clear sense of a global 'common home'. This intention continued through all his visits, even when silence was not the norm as it had been in Auschwitz and Japan, for his visits served to bring peace to those who were involved in wars and conflicts between and within nations.

Notes

1 It has been argued by historians that the Schism of 1054 on matters of pneumatology was aggravated by the pillage of Constantinople by Crusaders in 1204 who, rerouting from Jerusalem during the Fourth Crusade (1202) and over a period of two years, pillaged Constantinople, committing mass rape, murder, and looting of churches; see among other works Jonathan Philips, *The Fourth Crusade and the Sack of Constantinople*, New York: Viking, 2004, and Donald E. Queller and Thomas F. Madden, *The Fourth Crusade: The Conquest of Constantinople*, Philadelphia: University of Pennsylvania Press, 1999. For a comprehensive history of the crusades, see Jonathan Phillips, *The Crusades, 1095–1204*. London: Routledge, 2014.

2 John XXIII, *Pacem in Terris: Encyclical of Pope John XXIII on Establishing Universal Peace in Truth, Justice, Charity, and Liberty*. Vatican City: Librería Editrice Vaticana, 11 April 1963, §112.

3 Pope Francis visited Poland on the XXXI World Youth Day, 27–31 July 2016.

4 John Paul II, 'Speech at Auschwitz', 7 June 1979.

5 Benedict XVI, 'Address: Visit to the Auschwitz Camp', Auschwitz-Birkenau, 28 May 2006.

6 Benedict XVI, 'Address: Visit to the Auschwitz Camp', Auschwitz-Birkenau, 28 May 2006.

7 Mario I. Aguilar, *Religion, Torture and the Liberation of God*. New York: Routledge, 2015.

8 Fr Maximilian Kolbe died in Auschwitz as prisoner 16670 on 14 August 1941. As customary after a prisoner's escape the Nazis selected ten prisoners to be starved to death as communal and public punishment. One of those selected, Franciszek Gajowniczek, started screaming for his wife and children. Fr Kolbe requested to die instead of this man who was spared. Fr Kolbe went together with other nine to the death block of Building 13 where they all died of starvation. His body was cremated. Kolbe was beatified as Confessor by Paul VI in 1970 and canonised as Martyr by John Paul II in 1981; see Damien Walne and Joan Flory, *Totally Hers: St. Maximilian Kolbe*. High Wycombe, Bucks: Dites Publications, 1983.

9 I note here the issue of suicide by several important survivors of the Shoah, such as Benno Werzberger (Israel), Tadeusz Borowski (Poland), Paul Celan and Piotr Rawicz (Paris), Bruno Bettelheim (United States), and Primo Levi (Italy). The reflections by Elie Wiesel are quite pertinent to understand the extension of death by survivors and their despair at being isolated through their life witness; see Elie Wiesel, 'Three suicides', in *And the Sea Is Never Full: Memoirs 1969-*. London: HarperCollins, 2000, pp. 345–351.

10 For a fuller explanation of this silencing of the word, see Chapter 7: 'Silence, the pro-logos and the monk in Raimon Panikkar', in Mario I Aguilar, *Christian Ashrams, Hindu Caves and Sacred Rivers: Christian-Hindu Monastic Dialogue in India 1950–1993*, London and Philadelphia: Jessica Kingsley, 2016, pp. 143–158.

11 Raimon Panikkar, *Mysticism and Spirituality, Part Two: Spirituality, the Way of Life, Opera Omnia*, Vol. I.2, edited by M. Carrara Pavan. Maryknoll, NY: Orbis, 2014, p. 122.

12 Raimon Panikkar, *Opera Omnia*, Vol. I.2, p. 122.

13 Raimon Panikkar, 'Sūtra 3: Silence over the Word', *Opera Omnia*, Vol. I.2, pp. 163–166.

14 'Pope Francis visits Auschwitz-Birkenau Museum and Memorial', Vatican Radio, 29 July 2016.

15 'Memoria e silenzio: Durante la visita ad Auschwitz e Birkenau il Papa prega per le vittime della Shoah – L'invocazione al Signore e la richiesta di perdono per tanta crudeltà', *L'Osservatore Romano*, 30 July 2016.

16 The full two-hour video broadcasted by Vatican Television is available at https://www.youtube.com/watch?v=FO6OCefhNn4.

17 According to the information provided by the Memorial and Museum Auschwitz-Birkenau, 'the first and oldest was the so-called "main camp," later also known as "Auschwitz I" (the number of prisoners fluctuated around 15,000, sometimes rising above 20,000), which was established on the grounds and in the buildings of prewar Polish barracks. The second part was the Birkenau camp (which held over 90,000 prisoners in 1944), also known as "Auschwitz II". This was the largest part of the Auschwitz complex. The Nazis began building it in 1941 on the site of the village of Brzezinka, three kilometers from Oswiecim. The Polish civilian population was evicted and their houses confiscated and demolished. The greater part of the apparatus of mass extermination was built in Birkenau and the majority of the victims were murdered here'; see http://auschwitz.org/en/history/kl-auschwitz-birkenau/.

18 Fabrice d'Almeida, 'Prólogo', in Carl Schrade, ed., *El veterano: Once años en los campos de concentración nazis*. Barcelona: Ático de los libros, 2013, pp. 13–32 at p. 23.

19 http://www.yadvashem.org/yv/en/righteous/about.asp#!prettyPhoto.

20 Pope Francis, Tribute to the Martyr Saints, 'Greetings of His Holiness', Martyr's Monument, Nishizaka Hill (Nagasaki), Sunday 24 November 2019. Vatican City: Librería Editrice Vaticana.

21 'Video Message of the Holy Father Francis for his upcoming Apostolic Trip to Japan', Bulletin of the Holy See Press Office, 18 November 2019.

22 Years later on the message of the 2021 Word Day of Peace, Pope Francis completed his sense of 'a culture of dialogue' with an

extension, namely 'a culture of care' so that religion and religious leaders 'can play an indispensable role in handing on to their followers, and to society at large, the values of solidarity, respect for differences, and concerns for our brothers and sisters in need' – 'Message of His Holiness Pope Francis for the celebration of the 54th World Day of Peace', 1 January 2021 § 8. Vatican City: Librería Editrice Vaticana.

23 Apostolic Journey of His Holiness Pope Francis to Thailand and Japan, 19–26 November 2019, 'Address of the Holy Father on nuclear weapons', Atomic Bomb Hypocenter Park (Nagasaki), Sunday 24 November 2019. Vatican City: Librería Editrice Vaticana.

24 John XXIII, *Pacem in Terris* § 112–113.

25 Pope Francis referred to the establishment of a global fund to assist impoverished peoples drawn from military budgets already suggested by Pope Paul VI in 1964; see Paul VI, Journey to India, 'Address of Paul VI to the Press', Bombay, Friday 4 December 1964, and Paul VI, *Populorum Progressio: Encyclical of Pope Paul VI on the Development of Peoples*, 26 March 1967 § 51.

26 Pope Francis, Meeting for Peace, 'Address of the Holy Father', Peace Memorial Hiroshima, Sunday 24 November 2019. Vatican City: Librería Editrice Vaticana.

27 John XXIII, *Pacem in Terris* § 37, cf. § 87–88.

28 Paul VI, Visit of His Holiness Paul VI to the United Nations, 'Address of the Holy Father Paul VI to the United Nations Organization', Monday 4 October 1965, 10. Vatican City: Librería Editrice Vaticana.

29 Vatican II, Pastoral Constitution on the Church in the Modern World *Gaudium et* Spes, promulgated by His Holiness, Pope Paul VI on 7 December 1965 § 78.

3

INTERNATIONAL
MEDIATIONS

Papal visits and Vatican history

A papal visit outside Italy has been a common occurrence since Pope Paul VI, who, availing himself of the expansion of air commercial transport, visited Colombia for the Eucharistic Congress, opened the Second General Meeting of Latin American bishops in Medellin, and visited Uganda on the canonisation of the Ugandan martyrs, all within 1968. All those occasions contributed to a new understanding of the modern papacy as open to affirm the life of Catholic communities outside Europe and systematically strengthening diplomatic ties between the Vatican and countries that maintained diplomatic relations with the Holy See. The Vatican City State was founded in 1929 following the signing of the Lateran Pacts between the Holy See and Italy on 11 February 1929, and it was ratified on 7 June 1929, as a functioning contemporary state with its own ministries and with ambassadors (Apostolic Nuncios) throughout the world. John Paul II stressed the importance of papal visits to other states during his 25 years of pontificate, and Pope Francis provided a continuity to such visits. However, Pope Francis introduced his own choices within many invitations to visit by choosing to visit countries in which the Vatican had been particularly involved in processes of mediation, peace, and reconciliation, as well as countries where a minority Catholic population needed affirmation or further encouragement for interfaith dialogue. The visit to Cuba in 2015, for example, strengthened new horizons of cooperation between

DOI: 10.4324/9781003172345-4

Cuba and the United States as well as providing the first working meeting and mutual cooperation between a Pope and the Archbishop of Constantinople and Ecumenical Patriarch of the Orthodox Church (elected 1991), since the split of Churches of the East and the West in 1054.[1] By 2017 and his visit to Myanmar, Pope Francis had made ten apostolic visits outside Europe, with a visit to Chile and Peru (January 2018) following his visit to Myanmar.[2]

A papal visit has a complexity and intense preparation not spotted by the orderly arrival of Pope Francis, and there are several areas to be looked at by different teams, including security, health, luggage, and even presents that need to be prepared and given by Pope Francis during his visits. Pope Francis and his delegation, including invited journalists, fly out of Italy in Alitalia, and he is usually transported from country to country by the national airline of the state he is visiting. Speeches that constitute the main preparation of a papal visit comprise a mixture of continuity and historical issues to be remembered and new issues that are aired in public and usually discussed over a period in public.

In fact, Pope Francis is aware that whatever he is going to say could mark diplomatic relations between the state he is visiting and the Vatican in the future, and at the same time he needs to affirm Catholics and member of other faith communities within a country. Within such journeys, public teachings on issues that could be contextually central to the papal visit become central to a journey between the Pope as the head of the Vatican State as well as the Pope as the head of the global Catholic Church. Thus, in the case of the visit to Myanmar, the eyes of the global media were set on the moment when Pope Francis addressed the government of Myanmar wondering if he was to mention the persecution of the Rohingya by name in public. He did not, and the media declared this a papal failure. Pope Francis decided not to mention the Rohingya, as he told journalists on his way back to the Vatican, as not to 'slam the door' on the face of his hosts. However, he was satisfied that in his private meeting with Aung San Suu Kyi and Myanmar's powerful military chief, General Min Aung Hlaing, he had been heard.[3] Pope Francis defined a papal visit during his first journey outside Europe, to Brazil in

2013, when he said that a papal visit is 'for the good of society, the good of young people and the good of the elderly'.

It is a fact that most countries in the world have diplomatic relations with the Holy See and that heads of state regularly visit the Vatican to discuss with Pope Francis matters of common interest. Thus, when Pope Francis decides to visit another state, it is for serious and pressing reasons. For example, Pope Francis' visit to the United States in 2016 was a visit aimed at the affirmation of the Catholic communities after the scandals of child abuse by clergy, amid major discussions on the treatment of refugees, ongoing racial and religious divisions, and after the opening of diplomatic conversations between the United States and Cuba. The Pope cannot arrive in another country without the consent of the host government, and therefore common issues of interest are quickly established, and permissions granted either for a state visit, an apostolic visit, or a pastoral visit. For example, Pope Francis' visit to Myanmar required such permission, and, indeed, it must be recognised that Aung San Suu Kyi must have been instrumental in securing a positive response to the Vatican's request for a visit with the real possibility that the military command could have claimed that it was not safe at that time for Pope Francis to visit.

Peace in Colombia

It has not been unusual for popes to become involved in helping international partners to negotiate peace accords, and in the case of South American nations John Paul II had been central in the avoidance of a war between Chile and Argentina in the late 1970s with the signing of a peace treaty between Chile and Argentina.[4] Behind such requests or offers for mediation lay the moral authority given to the popes by a majority Roman Catholic population in Latin America and the advancement of a papal international presence advocated by John Paul II through his many visits over a long papacy.[5] In the case of the Colombian peace accord, Pope Francis was not directly involved in the public negotiations, but at the time when discussions had been difficult between the Fuerzas Armadas Revolucionarias de Colombia

(FARC) and the Colombian government his own encouragement created the conditions for a final agreement. Thus, according to the Italian historian Gianni La Bella, of the Saint Egidio Community in Rome, the FARC and the Colombian government recognised the authority of Pope Francis and committed themselves not to let the conversations collapse.[6]

The history of warfare in Colombia had been a long one. Such armed conflict was the longest in the world and began in 1964 with the formation of two guerrilla groups: the FARC and the ELN (Ejército de Liberación Nacional).[7] However, political violence in Colombia had taken place since the nineteenth century, particularly after the assassination of the Liberal Party presidential candidate, Jorge Gaitan in 1948, starting a decade of 200,000 killings, mainly of peasant farmers, known as *la Violencia*. After that period peasants started organising themselves advocating a reaction towards social injustice and the great economic inequality within that South American nation. Thus, the elites requested the government to end the existence of these groups in the south of the country, groups that established what became known as 'independent republics'. In 1964, the Colombian Army marched into the zone known as Marquetalia to find themselves fighting a guerrilla army rather than groups of peasants. In 1966 such guerrilla army became the FARC. At the same time, the ELN formed by university students who had returned from Cuba and who associated themselves with the Communist Party of Colombia was formed in 1964. The ELN had among their fighters the Catholic priest Camilo Torres, previously university chaplain who joined them and died in combat in San Vicente de Churcurí (15 February 1966). By the 1980s, paramilitary organisations associated to landowners and drug cartels were formed with the support of the Colombian state, a variety of organisations with a membership of 8,000 paramilitary soldiers who united themselves in 1997 under the Self-Defence Forces of Colombia (AUC). Over the years, thousands of Colombians died, were kidnapped, and experienced insecurity. Thus, the peace accord supported by Pope Francis was welcomed by all parties, and the FARC and the ELN became political parties in 2017.

The final agreement between those involved in the peace negotiations took place in 2015 with the help of Pope Francis. During his apostolic visit to Cuba (19–28 September 2015) and as an addendum to his formal homily during the Mass at the Plaza de la Revolución, Pope Francis addressed the Colombian government and the FARC and told them 'we don't have the right to allow another failure'.[8] In his formal homily, Pope Francis reiterated his sense that service becomes the central motto for any relations within Cuba and indeed other states so that 'the importance of a people, a nation, and the importance of individuals, which is always based on how they seek to serve their vulnerable brothers and sisters'.[9] In May and August 2015, Professor La Bella carried personally two letters from the FARC to Pope Francis, with the agreement of the Colombian government, requesting his involvement in the process, as they wanted peace. As a result, the Pope agreed to get publicly involved, but at the end there was no need for Pope Francis' direct involvement as the President of Colombia Juan Manuel Santos and the leader of the FARC, Timoleón Jiménez (aka Timochenko), agreed to sign a peace accord within a period of six months from the Pope's call for peace.

Uncovering the truth of abuse: Chile

However, the most difficult engagement of Pope Francis' pontificate was his visit to Chile, a majority Catholic country with a previously prophetic Church, that stood accused of covering abuse in a large scale while awaiting the papal visit. As a result of his visit, Pope Francis welcomed victims to the Vatican, and, within an *ad limina* visit of all Chilean bishops to the Vatican, he accepted their resignation leaving the Chilean bishops as the only ones in history to have been challenged and disgraced by Pope Francis' preference for the abused rather than for his own clerics. The Chilean bishops had covered abuse at a massive scale, and they had lied to Pope Francis during his visit.

Pope Francis recognised that the 'lowest moment of his pontificate' came on 18 January 2018 during his visit to Chile.[10] He was getting ready to attend the open-air Mass in Iquique, in the Chilean northern desert when a journalist asked him about Bishop Juan Barros, a Chilean bishop appointed by Pope Francis in 2015. He had been accused of covering abuse by Fr Fernando Karadima during the 1980s and 1990s, and Pope Francis' angry reply to accusing journalists was 'when you bring me proofs, we will talk'. In 2010, public accusations against Karadima, a well-known parish priest in the well-to-do neighbourhood of El Bosque, Providencia, Santiago had shocked Chilean public opinion. The details of such abuses were disgusting, but Bishop Barros had always defended Karadima. Thus, when Barros was appointed Bishop of Osorno lay people protested and blocked entrances and proceedings at the local cathedral, furiously attacking bishops who were attending the episcopal inauguration, including Bishop Pellegrin of Chillán, later accused of abuse as well.

I remember being in Chile for the Pope's visit standing at the main avenue where the papal car was to pass from the airport. Fr Mariano Puga, a worker priest who always lived poorly in shanty towns was protesting with the victims as Pope Francis' car left the airport for the Vatican Nunciature. There were disruptions at all places and a sense that at the Parque O'Higgins where I arrived very early for the Mass on the following day, there was going to be a poisoned atmosphere. And so it was. As Bishop Barros joined other bishops at the open-air Eucharist it felt as if nothing had ever happened. As the Mass ended, I left with a bitter sense that the previously prophetic Church of Cardinal Raúl Silva Henríquez who protected the poor and the marginalised against the abuses by the military had gone. It was a sad feeling rather than the public joy felt by Peruvians who welcomed Pope Francis in his visit to Peru a few days later. Bishop Barros became the centre of media attention rather than Pope Francis. Later, in June 2018, Bishop Barros stepped down from his post as Bishop of Osorno, together with Cristián Caro, Bishop of Puerto Montt, and Gonzalo Duarte, Bishop of Valparaíso.[11]

Three victims of abuse, James Hamilton, Andrés Murillo, and Juan Carlos Cruz, had claimed during Pope Francis' visit to Chile that his apology was empty and that they had not been heard in their request for truth and for the removal of the paedophile priests. Pope Francis admitted he was wrong in his support of Bishop Barros, and after commissioning a thorough investigation by allowing victims of abuse to come forward and be listened to by Archbishop Charles Scicluna of Malta, he realised that during his visit there had been an institutional cover-up. Archbishop Scicluna arrived in Santiago on 19 February 2018, and his aim was to listen to those who had any evidence about Bishop Barros' cover-up of abuse and indeed anybody who would like to see him about other cases of sexual abuse within the Catholic Church in Chile.[12] The Scicluna report covered systematic abuse not only by Karadima but also by priests and members of religious orders throughout Chile. On the part of the Chilean bishops, there was denial and suppression. For Pope Francis, there was not only abuse but also corruption, a perversion of power that was a threat to faith itself. Pope Francis invited Hamilton, Murillo, and Cruz to Rome. At the Casa Santa Marta, he listened to each one of them separately and then to three of them together while they stayed as his guests, and immediately moved to address the Chilean bishops. They had to go to Rome, all of them, and once they gathered Pope Francis read a ten-page letter in which he advised them to repent for their sins and indirectly asked for their resignation. In May 2018, they did in full, an unprecedented move within the history of the Catholic Church.

Thus, Pope Francis' visit to Chile, that was heralded as a pastoral visit and a return to a country where he studied as a young Jesuit, became an ecclesial mediation of great proportions, and Pope Francis' address to the Chilean clergy at the Santiago Cathedral was an example of such strong diplomacy but with the tools of a disarming spiritual director. Pope Francis guided his bishops away from any further actions arising out of their use of corrupt power. Pope Francis addressed clericalism as the wrong assumption that the Church is made of a consecrated elite rather than of the People of God so that 'the lack of consciousness of belonging to God's faithful people as servants, and not as masters, can lead us to one of the temptations that is most damaging to the missionary outreach that we are called to promote'.[13]

Peace visits to Myanmar and Bangladesh (2017)

It is difficult to argue if the problems with clerics in Chile were harder to deal with than Pope Francis' visit to Myanmar and Bangladesh at a time when the international community was outraged at the burning of Rohingya villages in Myanmar. While the Nobel Peace Prize winner, Aung San Suu Kyi, denied accusations of genocide against the Muslim Rohingya, Pope Francis visited Myanmar to celebrate the start of diplomatic relations between the Vatican and Myanmar. Pope Francis journeyed to Myanmar and Bangladesh from 26 November to 2 December 2017. The journey was a clear opportunity wanted by Pope Francis to foster efforts to protect the Muslims of Myanmar (Rohingya) who during 2017 had been once again attacked by government forces under state accusations of aiding guerrilla and terrorists. Under international language it was clear that ethnic cleansing was taking place under the eyes of the international community and with the alleged complicity of the Nobel Peace Prize winner Aung San Suu Kyi, then Madame Councillor of Myanmar.[14] The visit to Myanmar was combined with a short stop at Bangladesh, state that was the recipient of thousands of refugees and that through the aid of Muslim businessmen sheltered and fed Rohingya refugees. It is plausible to argue that the international media focused on the Pope's meeting with Aung San Suu Kyi and ignored the rest of the visit to Myanmar and Bangladesh. However, it was indeed through the presence of Aung Suu Kyi that the Vatican could exercise some influence simply because diplomatic relations between the Holy See and Myanmar had been recently agreed. Pope Francis had welcomed Aung San Suu Kyi to the Vatican in May 2017 to seal the opening of diplomatic relations between the Holy See and Myanmar to the level of an Apostolic Nunciature.[15] The purpose of the restoration of diplomatic relations was 'to promote bonds of mutual friendship'.[16]

Within this difficult political and international context, Pope Francis wanted to support safety for Rohingya in Myanmar and Bangladesh. At the same time, he needed to affirm the social identity and religious freedom of Catholic communities in both countries, communities that have been in recent times under scrutiny by both the Myanmar and the Bangladeshi government. Therefore, on the one hand the Pope faced the challenge of condemning the violence of Myanmar state agents while affirming the crucial role of the state of Bangladesh in the protection of Muslims and Christians alike. Pope Francis's visit put pressure on the Myanmar government affirming the life of Catholics in Myanmar within times of difficult discussions on the role and existence of religious minorities within a predominantly Buddhist country. The Pope continued his option for visits to places 'at the end of the earth' for a purpose and ventured within an Asian continent that remains for the Vatican central to the development of interfaith dialogue in the contemporary world.[17]

The 2017 'ethnic cleansing' of Rohingya in Myanmar started on 25 August when Myanmar military forces and extremist Buddhists began an attack on Rohingya villages. The narratives by the Myanmar government were known accusations that there were guerrilla forces operating in the area and that the Rohingya had no right to be within Myanmar as they were foreigners. Indeed, the statelessness of the Rohingya was settled by the Myanmar government in 1982 when Myanmar citizenship law did not include the Rohingya on the list of 135 recognised national ethnic groups (Chan). Thus, the Rohingya state problem is not one of solely faith but of nationality because by the fact of not being included among the national ethnic groups the Rohingya remained stateless and outside the boundaries of Myanmar state law. The Rohingya settled in the Arakan region between the fourteenth and eighteenth centuries, when the Arakanese city of Mrauk U, a key trading centre in Asia, was being ruled by Muslim sultans. However, the nationality laws passed by General Ne Win in 1982 assumed them as Bangladeshi and therefore as illegal immigrants.

On 28 August 2017, the Holy See Press Office confirmed Pope Francis' trip to Asia, and Vatican commentators speculated that he would surely visit India as Pope Francis had indicated that wish on 2 October 2016. On 29 July 2017, the Cardinal of Bangladesh confirmed that Pope Francis was to visit Bangladesh; however, Pope Francis' main destination was Myanmar. Reasons abounded: the India trip did not work out as, in the words of Pope Francis, 'the procedures became protracted' and therefore a trip to India was postponed. However, Pope Francis had an immediate concerned reaction towards the possible ethnic cleansing that supposedly was taking place in Myanmar. For public opinion, the Myanmar destination came as a surprise as no pope had previously visited the country, and there was ongoing violence in Myanmar at that moment.

The visit to Myanmar (27–30 November 2017)

As in most papal visits, Pope Francis recorded a video message to the people of Myanmar before starting his journey. Pope Francis extended his friendship to the people of Myanmar and highlighted the purpose of his visit as 'to confirm the Catholic community of Myanmar' in faith, faith that teaches 'the dignity of every man and woman, and that demands the care of the poorest and those most in need'. He also affirmed his visit as 'intended to build harmony and cooperation in the service of the common good' and spoke of building a 'single human family'. His purpose of interfaith dialogue was marked by his first meeting in Myanmar with religious leaders at Archbishop's House on the morning of the 28 November 2017. Thus, the Pope's arrival took place at Yangon on the previous day of his meeting with the Myanmar government. During that first day in Myanmar, Pope Francis met with religious leaders, and, a day later, he departed for Nay Pyi Taw for his meeting with the Myanmar political authorities. This was a significant departure from Vatican protocols in which a meeting with the head of state or a senior minister takes place on arrival while public celebrations of the Eucharist and meetings with other religious leaders happen after the start of a state visit. The same protocol is also used within state visits to the Vatican where Pope Francis usually meets on arrival and walks heads of state to his library rather than waiting for them. Thus, the change of protocol could have indicated the difficulties that Myanmar was having with foreign governments that had become extremely critical of the violence used against the minority Muslim population in Myanmar. Such difficulties were mediated through Pope Francis' meeting with religious leaders, mostly Buddhists.

After visiting the President of the government, the Madam State Councillor, and the Union Minister for Foreign Affairs, Pope Francis met with authorities, civil society, and the diplomatic corps at the International Convention Centre. Those one-to-one conversations remain confidential. However, in the plane on his way back from Myanmar and Bangladesh Pope Francis told reporters that his choice had been to speak about human rights in general when in public so that he could speak more frankly in private. Nevertheless, Pope Francis expressed his opinion that his message supporting the Muslim minorities had been heard by Aung San Suu Kyi and Myanmar's powerful military chief, General Min Aung Hlaing. The general had asked for a meeting, and later Pope Francis described the conversation as a nice one, in which he did not negotiate the truth and in which Pope Francis clearly spoke of new journeys rather than old ones.

At the public and televised meeting that followed, the Madame Councillor delivered a well-rehearsed speech with citations from the Gospel and words in Italian. From the start she recognised Myanmar's 'faith in the power and possibility of peace and loving kindness'. Citing from the Myanmar national anthem and the will of the nations' fathers, including her own father, she accepted that 'true freedom cannot survive without justice'. She described Myanmar as a land of opportunity and as 'a rich tapestry of different peoples, languages and religions, woven on a backdrop of vast natural potential'. However, she recognised the difficulties that lie ahead on the road to peace (Nationwide Ceasefire Agreement) to be reinforced by the attainment of sustainable development. She accepted that the challenging situation of the Rakhine had been the focus of the world's attention with longstanding issues to be resolved between the different communities in the Rakhine. The Christian-educated Buddhist thanked Pope Francis for bringing compassion and encouragement, and she recalled the words by Pope Francis on the celebration of the 50th World Day of peace (1 January 2017): 'Jesus himself offers a "manual" for this strategy of peacemaking in the Sermon of the

Mount. The eight Beatitudes (cf. Mt. 5:3–10) provide a portrait of the person we could describe as blessed, good and authentic'. She further thanked Pope Francis for his visit to Myanmar after six months of the establishment of diplomatic relations with the Vatican. She recalled the start of her education at St Francis Convent in Rangoon, and she even joked that she was entitled to more blessings from Pope Francis but that such blessings as usual would be shared throughout Myanmar. And even through the difficult moments she encountered within the papal visit she outlined her own dream of a lifetime as 'to leave to the future a people united and at peace, secure in their capacity to grow and prosper in a changing world […] always ready to hold out a helping hand to those in need'. Finally, she expressed her thanks for the Catholic Church's children who were also part of Myanmar in a common journey ('*Continuiamo a camminare insieme con fiducia*').

In his own speech Pope Francis acknowledged the kind words of the Madam State Councillor and reiterated that he was visiting the Catholic community to strengthen their commitment to the common good as well as strengthening the diplomatic relations between the Vatican and Myanmar that had been restored during Pope Francis' pontificate. Pope Francis stressed the internal conflicts and violence that had occurred and suggested that 'the healing of those wounds must be a paramount political and spiritual priority'. He ventured to suggest that 'the future of Myanmar must be peace, a peace based on respect for the dignity and rights of each member of society, respect for each ethnic group and its identity, respect for the rule of law, and respect for a democratic order that enables each individual and every group – none excluded – to offer its legitimate contribution to the common good'. Furthermore, in such a process of reconciliation, religious communities have an important role to play, according to Pope Francis, 'repairing the emotional, spiritual and psychological wounds of those who have suffered in the years of conflict'.

On the following day, 29 November 2017, Pope Francis presided a Mass at Kyaikkasan Ground, a meeting with the Supreme

'Sangha' Council of Buddhist Monks at the Kaba Aye Centre and a meeting with Catholic bishops of Myanmar in the Hall of St Mary's Cathedral. On 30 November 2017, Pope Francis presided a Mass with the youth at St Mary's Cathedral in Yangon, and after an official farewell he departed for Dhaka.

Bangladesh: ecclesiastical and political history

The visit to Myanmar was a challenging one because of the international media scrutiny around the papal visit and what he was going to say about the ethnic cleansing of Rohingya. However, the papal visit to Bangladesh which did not become central to media coverage was an even more challenging one. The history of partition from India and the ever-increasing centrality of Islam was also a challenge for a papal visit, particularly to a state that had welcomed and supported the Rohingya from Myanmar. The history of Bangladesh originated in the 1947 Partition of India when in August British India became independent in the form of two separate nations: India and Pakistan, and Hindus and Muslims separated. Within the 1947 partition of India, the province of Bengal became two: West Bengal that remained within India and East Bengal that became the eastern part of Pakistan, known after 1955 as East Pakistan. The introduction of Urdu as a national language in Pakistan created animosity among Bengali-speaking citizens of East Pakistan, and after the elections of 1971 and the intervention of the Pakistani and Indian armies East Pakistan became Bangladesh with its capital in Dhaka. A self-declared secular nation in the line of India, Bangladesh constitutionalism chose secularism contextually meaning the coexistence of religions rather than European secularisation with the absence of religion at the core of the public engagement with the polis.

The papal visit to Bangladesh was linked to the Rohingya crisis, but it also showed a Vatican renewed interest for the region of India-Pakistan-Bangladesh that was reinforced when at the Consistory of 29 June 2018 Pope Francis made His Excellency

Joseph Coutts, Archbishop of Karachi, a new Cardinal of the Roman Catholic Church.[18]

The visit to Bangladesh
(30 November–2 December 2017)

On arrival in Dhaka, Pope Francis visited the National Martyr's Memorial of Savar, taking part in a homage to the Father of the Nation at Bangabandhu Memorial Museum and signing the Book of Honour. After a courtesy visit to the President in the presidential palace, Pope Francis had a meeting with government and civil authorities and the diplomatic corps at the presidential palace. On Friday 1st December 2017 and on his second day in Bangladesh Pope Francis presided a public Mass at Suhrawardy Udyan Park in which he presided over ordinations to the priesthood. Later that day, he received the visit of the Prime Minister at the Apostolic Nunciature and visited the Cathedral.

One of the central moments of his visit was the meeting with the bishops of Bangladesh at the home for retired priests. On entering the place, Pope Francis was asked to say a few words and through those words he encouraged evangelisation not as proselytising but as witness stating very clearly that evangelisation 'means showing by our words and our lives the treasure we have received'. During his meetings with the bishops of Bangladesh he praised their 1985 Pastoral Plan centred on *communion*. However, he stressed the importance of a *ministry of presence* not for the sake of being seen but in the sense of God's *condescension* following the incarnation of the one among us.

Later, and on the same day, Pope Francis led an ecumenical and interreligious meeting for peace at the Garden of the Archbishop's residence. That interfaith meeting was marked by the words of Pope Francis to the Rohingya in which he asked them personally for their forgiveness: 'In the name of everyone, of those who persecute you, of those who have wronged you, above all for the indifference of the world, I ask your forgiveness. Forgiveness'. Furthermore, in explaining human beings as God's creation, in his image, he outlined the dignity of the Rohingya as an image of God. However, the words that the world was waiting for came during this short speech when Pope Francis acknowledged the rights of the Rohingya:

> Let us continue to work actively for the recognition of their rights. Let us not close our hearts or look the other way. The presence of God, today, is also called "Rohingya". May each of us respond in his or her own way.

During that meeting Pope Francis asked the religious leaders and faith communities to remember the right to religious freedom that had been inbuilt in the foundation of Bangladesh and the opportunity that faith communities had to contribute to the building of peace together. He spoke about a 'culture of encounter' which to operate needed an 'openness of heart' based on some essential features such as a *door* to others and a *ladder* that reaches up to the Absolute.[19] Furthermore, he told those present that an openness of heart is a *path* that leads to the pursuit of goodness, justice, and solidarity. He thanked the religious communities of Bangladesh for promoting such a 'culture of encounter' for taking care of the common house, the environment, and the planet.

On his third and last day in Bangladesh, Pope Francis paid a private visit to Tejgaon Mother Theresa House and had a meeting with priests, religious, consecrated men and women, seminarians, and novices at the Holy Rosary Church. As customary, Pope Francis had an eight-page speech that he decided not to read but gave to Cardinal Rosario to be translated into Bengali and to be circulated to all those attending the meeting. He spoke without a script about unity in the community and about the example of interfaith dialogue set by Bangladesh. However, he warned them against the first enemy to unity, namely gossip, so much a part of all communities, including those members of communities of priests, bishops, and those in consecrated life. While the speech could be considered secondary to those given to the unity of a nation and of larger international affairs, Pope Francis settled the example needed of those consecrated Catholics within a larger perspective. Thus, without unity, Christians and other faith communities will not contribute to larger issues of international affairs, such as the challenges to discrimination according to ethnicity and history, as it has been the case of Myanmar, India, Pakistan, and Bangladesh. He visited the Christian cemetery and the old church and later met with the youth at the Notre Dame College in Dhaka leaving Bangladesh after an official farewell at the airport.

Notes

1 Since 2015 Pope Francis and Patriarch Bartholomew have gone together to pray in Lampedusa and have attended together the 500th anniversary of the Protestant Reformation in Sweden (2016). They both share a theological interest on ecological issues; see Pope Francis who cites Patriarch Bartholomew in *Laudato Si'* § 8–9.

2 Brazil (July 2013); Holy Land and Jordan (May 2014); Korea (August 2014); Turkey (November 2014); Sri Lanka and the Philippines (January 2015); Ecuador, Bolivia, and Paraguay (July 2015); Cuba, the United States, and the United Nations in New York (September 2015); Kenya, Uganda, and the Central African Republic (November 2015); Mexico (February 2016); Egypt (April 2017); and Colombia (September 2017).

3 See ITV News 3 December 2017, video available at http://www. itv.com/news/2017-12-03/pope-francis-explains-why-he-omitted-rohingya-from-myanmar-speech/

4 See Acta de Montevideo 8 January 1979. In 1987, Pope Francis visited Uruguay, Chile, and Argentina, to celebrate the peace accord between Chile and Argentina that had been achieved through the mediation of the Vatican and signed by the parties involved at the Palacio Taranco of Montevideo; see Viaje Apostólico a Uruguay, Chile y Argentina, 'Discurso del Santo Padre Juan Pablo II para conmemorar los acuerdos de Montevideo', Palacio Taranco de Montevideo, martes 31 de marzo de 1987. Vatican City: Librería Editrice Vaticana.

5 Vicente Enrique Tarancón, Eduardo Martínez Somalo, José Antonio Infantes Florido y otros, *Juan Pablo II y nuestro tiempo*. Tomo I: Quien es Juan Pablo II, un hombre de Dios al servicio de los hombres. Tomo II: Los mil días del Papa Wojtyla. Tomo III: Los viajes de Juan Pablo II. Madrid: Mateu Cromo, 1992.

6 'Papa Francisco fue "clave" para acuerdo de paz en Colombia', La Información España 24 September 2015 at Papa Francisco fue "clave" para acuerdo de paz en Colombia (lainformacion.com), accessed 17 January 2021.

7 James J. Brittain, *Revolutionary Social Change in Colombia: The Origin and Direction of the FARC-EP*. London and New York: Pluto, 2010; Johanna Higgs, *Militarized Youth: The Children of the*

FARC. New York: Palgrave Macmillan, 2020; and Garry Leech, *The FARC: The Longest Insurgency.* London: Zed Books, 2011.

8 '"No tenemos derecho a permitirnos otro fracaso", dice papa Francisco sobre diálogos de paz entre el gobierno de Colombia y las FARC', BBC Mundo 20 September 2015 at "No tenemos derecho a permitirnos otro fracaso", dice papa Francisco sobre diálogos de paz entre el gobierno de Colombia y las FARC – BBC News Mundo.

9 Apostolic Journey of His Holiness to Cuba, to the United States of America, and visit to the United Nations Headquarters (19–28 September 2015), 'Holy Mass: Homily of His Holiness Pope Francis', Plaza de la Revolución, Havana, Sunday 20 September 2015. Vatican City: Librería Editrice Vaticana.

10 Austen Ivereigh, *Wounded Shepherd: Pope Francis and His Struggle to Convert the Catholic Church,* New York: Henry Holt and Company, 2019, p. 104. The papal visit included Chile and Peru and took place between 15 and 22 January 2018.

11 'El Papa Francisco acepta la renuncia de Juan Barros y otros dos obispos de Chile tras escándalo de abusos sexuales de menores', BBC News Mundo 11 June 2018 at El papa Francisco acepta la renuncia de Juan Barros y otros dos obispos de Chile tras escándalo de abusos sexuales de menores – BBC News Mundo.

12 Arzobispado de Santiago, 'Monseñor Charles Scicluna in Chile', Monday 19 February 2018 at Monseñor Charles Scicluna en Chile (iglesiadesantiago.cl).

13 Apostolic Journey of His Holiness Pope Francis to Chile and Peru (15–22 January 2018); meeting with the bishops, 'Greeting of the Holy Father', Santiago Cathedral Sacristy, Tuesday 16 January 2018.

14 Aung San Suu Kyi, the First State Councillor of Myanmar and who assumed office on 6 April 2006, was born on 19 June 1945 and received the Nobel Prize for Peace in 1991. She is the youngest daughter of Aung San, Father of the Nation of modern Myanmar. She was born in British Burma and graduated from the University of Delhi (1964) and the University of Oxford (1968). She worked at the United Nations for three years and married the Tibetan scholar Michael Aris in 1972 and they had two children. She became prominent during the 1988 uprisings and became the General Secretary of the National League for Democracy (NLD) which she formed with some retired generals. In the 1990s elections the NLD won 81% of the general votes, but the military refused to hand over power. She was already under house arrest and remained under house arrest for periods at a time totalling 15 years between 1989 and 2010.

15 Vatican and Burma establish full diplomatic relations', *Catholic Herald* 4 May 2017 at http://catholicherald.co.uk/news/2017/05/04/vatican-and-burma-establish-full-diplomatic-relations/.

16 Holy See Press Office, 'Comunicato della Sala Stampa: Allaccia-
mento delle Relazioni Diplomatiche tra la Repubblica dell'Unione
del Myanmar e la Santa Sede, 04.05.2017' B0296, 00672-EN.01
[English translation].

17 Pope Francis in his first appearance as elected Bishop of Rome told
the crowds: 'You know that it was the duty of the Conclave to give
Rome a Bishop. It seems that my brother Cardinals have gone to the
ends of the earth to get one'.

18 The countries with whom the Holy See does not have diplomatic
relations or a representation are the Kingdom of Bhutan, the Republic of the Maldives, the People's Republic of China, and the
Democratic People's Republic of Korea (otherwise known as North
Korea).

19 I note here that Pope Francis introduces within his speeches the
term Absolute used by Hinduism instead of God. This is significant
for interfaith dialogue, and it has been used not only by a pope but
by those Catholic monks living very close to Hinduism in India
during the twentieth century.

4

PEACE AND THE CARE OF
THE PLANET

If papal visits, as outlined in the previous chapter, were occasions in which Pope Francis visited a particular country or community to mediate peace and understanding, his thought and philosophy of the planet and the order of things became a prominent theme of a central dialogue with the contemporary world in search for the common good.[1] Pastoral or state visits constitute occasions in which central ideas and understandings of the Christian texts and traditions can be emphasised and put across. Indeed, the teaching office of a bishop and that of Pope Francis as the Bishop of Rome are central to the communion and unity of the Catholic Church, one part of which is the Roman (Latin) Catholic Church.[2] Thus, in his meeting with the Romanian authorities (2019), Pope Francis addressed political negotiations as follows: *To move forward together, as a way of shaping the future, requires a noble willingness to sacrifice something of one's own vision or best interest for the sake of a greater project, and thus to create a harmony that makes it possible to advance securely towards shared goals.*[3]

Encyclicals became part of Pope Francis' pastoral signature between 2013 and 2020. Encyclicals have been since the ancient Roman times of the Church letters sent by a bishop to the different churches around (ἐνκύκλιος circular). Encyclicals become letters with a theme of concern to a local bishop and, therefore, to Pope Francis as the bishop of Rome. Different than apostolic exhortations, apostolic constitutions, or apostolic letters, an encyclical constitutes a personal papal statement of interest and as

DOI: 10.4324/9781003172345-5

such indicates publicly a teaching being explored and given importance by a local bishop. Encyclicals become the signature of a pontificate in that they connect with the previous extension of the Tradition (as opposed to tradition as custom) and expand on themes of importance for the development of such Tradition as ecclesial teaching. Thus, encyclicals since the time of *Rerum Novarum* (Leo XIII, 1891) and the start of the social encyclicals have given directives vis-à-vis contemporary issues and Catholic Church' policies such as the condemnation of nuclear weapons (John XXIII, *Pacem in Terris*, 1963), the rejection of private property as a challenge to the common good, and the overcoming of nationalism and racism (Paul VI, *Populorum Progressio*, 1967). Once an announcement of an encyclical is made there is an expectation of an important pronouncement of policy and international engagement such as hunger, the condemnation of war, and the dialogue with secularism.

Pope Francis provided a continuity of his papacy with that of Benedict XVI by his first encyclical *Lumen Fidei* (29 June 2013).[4] The text was revised and completed from a full draft text on faith written by Benedict XVI coinciding with the 'Year of Faith' (2012–2013) and the 50th anniversary of the opening of the Second Vatican Council (1962–1965).[5] Thus, Pope Francis wrote: 'These considerations on faith – in continuity with all the Church's magisterium has pronounced on this theological virtue – are meant to supplement what Benedict XVI had written in his encyclical letters on charity and hope'.[6] The 'Year of Faith' concluded with a Mass presided by Pope Francis with the Patriarchs and Major Archbishops of the Eastern Catholic Churches present. Pope Francis in his homily reminded those present that 'Christ is *the centre of the people of God*' referring clearly to the continuity of such year of faith with the Second Vatican Council, and the definition of the Church as the people of God rather than solely as the baptised within the Roman Catholic Church.[7] For *Lumen Gentium*, as the dogmatic constitution on the Catholic Church of Vatican II, had stressed the connection between a people that followed God rather than the privileges of a few, the messianic people of God, so that 'God, however, does not make men [and women] holy and save them merely as individuals, without bond or link between one another'.[8] It is this idea of common solidarity and the common good rather than an individual salvation that Pope Francis was to develop on his second encyclical, his first manifesto to the world. The theme was going to be ecological, including the common house and the care of the planet.

Encyclical letter Laudato Si' (2015)

Laudato Si' (LS) became the first manifesto of intent by Pope Francis, and the impact of his dialogue with Patriarch Bartholomew who had written on the same themes became apparent.[9] However, the figure of St Francis of Assisi became central to understand the connections between the care of the planet and the Christian, human, and universal vocation of being human.[10] The genesis of the encyclical text can be traced back to a moment in which Pope Francis asked Cardinal Peter Turkson to prepare a draft of environmental realities and ecological concerns which Pope Francis could work with after. Peter Turkson had been at the centre of discussions on the environment as President of the Pontifical Council for Justice and Peace (2009–2017), and Pope Francis named him the first Prefect of the Dicastery for the Promotion of Integral Human Development (1 January 2017). Indeed, Turkson's influence was acknowledged by several writers working on ecological issues by inviting him to endorse their work through the writing of diverse prefaces of works on ecology, work, and the social doctrine of the Church. However, in that very genesis of Laudato Si' (August 2014) Turkson handed a very long first draft.[11]

LS is an encyclical that responds to the Catholic Tradition through its very name, that is, the Canticle of the Creatures of St Francis of Assisi, 'Praise be to you my Lord', the saint loved by Italians whose name Cardinal Jorge Mario Bergoglio took as the patron of his pontificate.[12] For Pope Francis, 'Saint Francis is the example *par excellence* of care for the vulnerable and of an integral ecology lived out joyfully and authentically'.[13] At the same time *LS* is a radical announcement of a shared humanity in a 'common home' that is 'like a sister with whom we share our life and a beautiful mother who opens her arms to embrace us'.[14] However, our common home 'now cries to us because of the harm we have inflicted on her by our irresponsible use and abuse of the goods with which God has endowed her'.[15] Using indigenous populations' language Pope Francis acknowledged climate change as a factor that is human-made so that 'the violence present in our hearts, wounded by sin, is also reflected in the symptoms of sickness evident in the soil, in the water, in the air and in all forms of life'.[16]

Pope Francis acknowledged that there were previous papal pronouncements on the planet, the environment, and ecology.[17] First, through *LS* Pope Francis intended to address all men and women of goodwill as Pope John XXIII did on the brink of nuclear war in 1963 through *Pacem in Terris*.[18] Later, John XXIII warned about unchecked human activity in *Octogesima Adveniens* (1971) stating vis-à-vis nature that 'humanity runs the risk of destroying it and becoming in turn a victim of this degradation'.[19] John XXIII had also warned the Food and Agriculture Organization of the United Nations about an 'ecological catastrophe' because of 'industrial civilisation'.[20] John Paul II in his first encyclical Redemptor Hominis (1979) commented on human beings who frequently saw in their natural environment only 'immediate use and consumption'.[21] Later, John Paul II called for a global ecological conversion.[22] For John Paul II argued that 'little effort had been made to "safeguard the moral conditions for an authentic human ecology".'[23] Benedict XVI challenged the inability of the world economy for 'correcting models of growth which have proved incapable of ensuring respect for the environment'.[24]

The ongoing friendship and respect by Pope Francis towards Patriarch Bartholomew is also outlined in his wish for 'full communion' and in the inclusion of Bartholomew's thought in the outlining of evidence and ultimately the Tradition of the Church.[25] For Bartholomew, the destruction of the planet is a sin, for 'to commit a crime against the natural world is a sin against ourselves and a sin against God'.[26] For Bartholomew showed a radical sense of God's presence in the world so that 'as Christians, we are also called "to accept the world as a sacrament of communion, as a way of sharing with God and our neighbours on a global scale".'[27]

At the centre of *LS* is Pope Francis' wish for the care of the planet with 'the urgent challenge to protect our common home [that] includes a concern to bring the whole human family together to seek a sustainable and integral development, for we know that things can change'.[28] Such utopia based on the always-present Creator brings hope to others, and, as a result, Pope Francis insisted on giving copies of *LS* to all official visitors to the Vatican in order to seek change regardless of challenging market economies and financial interests in the contemporary world. Indeed, the words of *LS* resonated over the years with people of no faith because they also had a humanist concern for the environment. Thus, on his visit to Cuba and on 20 September 2015 Pope Francis met the former Cuban leader Fidel Castro for 30 minutes at Fidel's home and gave him copies of *LS* and *Evangelii Gaudium*.[29] Both of them exchanged views on the environment, a topic that had not been known to be of interest to the Cuban leader.

The message of *LS* followed that of *Evangelii Gaudium* criticising the notion that markets generate wealth for all people. Thus, the deniers of climate change and its effects were extremely concerned about the Pope's attack on markets and industry in the United States, that naturally would attract wider attacks on capitalism and consumerism. Indeed, Pope Francis became a challenging critic of many given associations between capitalism, wealth, and the life of the Gospel in the United States. It is plausible to argue that Pope Francis used the same thought process he had used in the Aparecida document (2007), in which he had been the main redactor, mainly the see–judge–act means of reading an ecclesial document. In May 2007, the Latin American Bishops met in Aparecida, Brazil to deliberate about the life of the Catholic Church in Latin America, and already in its opening speech Benedict XVI reminded those present that the promises of fulfilment by Marxism and Capitalism were false.[30] Thus, as expected, Pope Francis cited from *LS* on his visit to the United States and his address to the joint session of the U.S. Congress reminding them of his call 'for a courageous and responsible effort to "redirect our steps", and to avert the most serious effects of the environmental deterioration caused by human activity'.[31] Such thoughts were reproduced from Pope Francis' address to the European Parliament where the previous year he had challenged the centrality of technology rather than humanity stating that 'to our dismay we see technical and economic questions dominating political debate, to the detriment of genuine concern for human beings'.[32]

LS became the most widely read papal document in history because it was not only a papal document, it also reproduced data from science that had been researched properly with a clear argument addressed to all within and outside the Church.[33] Thus, Chapter 1 presented data on what was happening to the 'common home'.[34] Constant and rapid change was taking place, change 'not necessarily geared to the common good or to integral and sustainable human development'.[35] Pollution, waste, and a throwaway culture has become a way of life, 'a throwaway culture which affects the excluded just as it quickly reduces things to rubbish'.[36] For 'the climate is a common good, belonging to all and meant for all', Pope Francis affirmed, and further, that it 'is a global problem with grave implications: environmental, social, economic, political and for the distribution of goods'.[37]

Pope Francis isolated not only a sound scientific analysis from scientific advisors but stressed also on areas of global concern, such as water scarcity, within 'the depletion of natural resources'.[38] However, the causes of such lack of biodiversity relate, according to Pope Francis, to 'short-sighted approaches to the economy, commerce and production'.[39] In *LS*, every aspect of the 'common home' is connected, and human beings as well as animals, plants, birds, and forests are affected by the expansion of cities that become 'unhealthy to live in'.[40] Global inequality does exist, and it is related to the use of raw resources from the Global South over a period of time. It is in the Global South where the most important reserves of the biosphere are found, 'yet access to ownership of goods and resources for meeting vital needs is inhabited by a system of commercial relations and ownership which is structurally perverse'.[41] It is here that Pope Francis links the care of the planet with the care of the poor rather than with solely technology and finance.[42]

Even when accepting different opinions and diverse discussions on the common home, Pope Francis also advanced the Christian foundation of a care for the planet within a framework of faith in a Creator.[43] Pope Francis dedicated a period of intense five years (2015–2020) to the task of alerting humanity to the care of the 'common home' until in 2020 he surprised the Church and the world with an extension of *LS*, namely the encyclical *Fratelli Tutti* (*FT*), on the themes of fraternity and social friendship.[44]

Encyclical letter Fratelli Tutti (2020)

On 3rd October 2020 and at the tomb of St Francis in Assisi, Pope Francis signed this new encyclical on fraternity and social friendship. In his first trip outside Rome since the start of the 2020 pandemic, Pope Francis entered the crypt where St Francis is buried and celebrated a private Mass attended by around 20 people. After the reading of the Gospel, he sat in silence, and after the Mass he thanked three Vatican officials who had collaborated with the transition of the original Spanish text. He then signed the text which launched publicly on the following day in Rome.[45] Fratelli Tutti (*FT*) written within the time of the European pandemic emphasises the darkness that created the possibility of people injured by the road, people discarded by society, and the possibility of confusion, loneliness, and desolation (Chapter 1). Pope Francis argued that it is at that moment when an injured stranger is at the side of the road that we can assume two different attitudes: we can continue our journey, or we can stop. We will be defined by that choice (Chapter 2). However, because God is love we are called to a universal fraternity, an openness to all. In fact, there no 'others' but only 'us'. Thus, we want an open world, a world without walls, without borders, without people rejected, without strangers (Chapter 3). The requirement for such an open world is an open heart through which we experience social friendship, seek what is morally good, as a practice and social ethic, because we are part of a universal fraternity. It could be argued that Pope Francis developed such a broad theory connecting socio-religious and humanitarian globalised ideas in

Chapters 4–6 of Fratelli Tutti to develop clear avenues of human fraternity based on justice for all and for all religions.

But for such conviction that all human beings are brothers and sisters not to remain an abstract idea 'numerous related issues emerge, forcing us to see things in a new light and to develop new responses'.[46] Pope Francis starts his very practical analysis of those borders and their limits with the reality of an immigrant.[47] Until the situation of the immigrant's home countries improve and we are responsible to help in that improvement as well, Pope Francis argues for our response to immigrants as follows: 'welcome, protect, promote, and integrate'.[48] The concreteness of steps outlined by Pope Francis is comprehensive and includes 'increasing and simplifying the granting of visas, opening humanitarian corridors for the most vulnerable refugees, providing suitable and dignified housing, the possibility of opening bank accounts and the guarantee of the minimum needed to survive'.[49] It is a clear call to action in very concrete terms towards immigrants without distinction or those persecuted because of political reasons or those who start a journey towards Europe because their conditions are of extreme poverty, displacement, war, or complete despair.

Indeed, Pope Francis is speaking about human beings who are part of that human fraternity rather than people who are trying to abuse the system of entry and residence in Europe. One could say that his visit to Lampedusa in 2013 had already prepared such disagreement between some states within the European government and the policies of welcoming, support, and integration fostered by the Vatican, a state which is not a member of the European Union. For at Lampedusa Pope Francis spoke of the sin of indifference so that 'in this globalized world, we have fallen into globalized indifference. We have become used to the suffering of others: it doesn't affect me; it doesn't concern me; it's none of my business!'[50] If the visit to Lampedusa was a self-awareness and an act of embracing the immigrants, particularly those from Africa, in his visit to Bari in February 2020, Pope Francis encouraged the bishops of the Mediterranean to fulfil the commandment of 'love thy neighbour and enemies' in the only way expected: a radical one, a

Christian one.[51] Thus, Pope Francis reminded the bishops of the Mediterranean gathered at Bari on that day about the important features of a Christian life saying, 'what use is a society of constant technological progress, if it becomes increasingly indifferent to its members in need? In preaching the Gospel, we hand on a way of thinking that respects each person by our unremitting effort to make the Church, the Churches, a sign of special care for the vulnerable and the poor'.[52] Furthermore, at the Eucharist celebrated on that day Pope Francis reminded participants of the radical call of the Gospel, a different call than other calls within society with these prophetic words: *Where the command of universal love is concerned, let us not accept excuses or preach prudent caution. The Lord was not cautious; he did not yield to compromises. He asks of us the extremism of charity. This is the only legitimate kind of Christian extremism: the extremism of love.*[53]

Full citizenship comes into the discussion within *FT* based on an equality of rights and duties so that all can enjoy justice.[54] For Pope Francis spoke clearly in several journeys about 'the discriminatory use of the term *minorities*', a term that creates feelings of isolation and inferiority.[55] However, Pope Francis is conscious that such difficulties cannot be solved by a single state but from a common effort by the international community so that 'global governance' comes into effect.[56] Thus, the arrival of immigrants can be a gift so that 'migrants bring an opportunity for enrichment and the integral human development of all'.[57] Thus, international cooperation in the context of globalisation requires, according to Pope Francis, a global juridical, political, and economic order that as outlined by Benedict XVI 'can increase and give direction to international cooperation for the development of all peoples in solidarity'.[58] Access to decision-making and the international markets would be necessary in that global order; however, by no means in a utilitarian manner but also with room for gratuitousness open to others.[59]

Gratuitousness becomes a possibility and 'makes it possible for us to welcome the stranger, even though this brings us no immediate tangible benefit'.[60] Otherwise the world becomes a 'frenetic commerce' in which there is a constant weight of what we give and what we receive in return.[61] It is within this section that Pope Francis outlines the clear guidelines of the Gospel and where the reader starts feeling that to follow his reflections is to clash head on with an economic global system that does not reflect the values of the Gospel. God gives freely, and this is the Gospel model.[62] Therefore, countries show their worth by thinking as part of a larger family.[63] Thus, narrow forms of nationalism 'are an extreme expression of an inability to grasp the meaning of their gratuitousness'.[64]

Within *FT* Pope Francis not only outlines clear Catholic positions towards contemporary issues such as the death penalty but also develops his master stroke of international cooperation: religions at the service of fraternity in the world.[65] Thus, his *address to discussions on war and the death penalty.*[66] Already John XXIII in *Pacem in Terris* (1963) had argued that 'it no longer makes sense to maintain that war is a fit instrument with which to repair the violation of justice', a substantial point taken by Pope Francis.[67] Particularly, Pope Francis requests that the narratives of victims be heard at all times so that war is rejected as a solution because it 'is a failure of politics and of humanity, a shameful capitulation, a stinging defeat before the forces of evil'.[68] The same principles of human failure and non-solution applies to the issue of deterrence with nuclear, chemical, or biological weapons, particularly within asymmetric issues of cybernetics and terrorism.[69] Pope Francis not only had already asked nations of the world to sign a treaty on non-deterrence when addressing the United Nations in 2017 but also had advocated, following Paul VI, the creation of a global fund to alleviate poverty and foster development with the money saved on the production and purchase of arms of deterrence, including nuclear weapons.[70]

Thus, through a wide range of initiatives, including papal visits, personal encounters, and documents to be discussed in the ecclesial, academic, and political world, Pope Francis has pointed to instruments of peace as a peacemaker. Thus, on the issue of the death penalty he has followed the Catholic Church's tradition on condemning such practice. John Paul II had already stated firmly that the death penalty 'is inadequate from a moral standpoint and no longer necessary from that of penal justice'.[71] However, John Paul II allowed for some cases by civil authorities' judgement while Pope Francis made the death penalty 'inadmissible' and the change was made to number 2267 of the *Catechism*.[72] And as indicated to all bishops of the Catholic Church in 2018, 'the Catholic Church is firmly committed to calling for its abolition worldwide'.[73]

The role of religious peacemaking

Within *FT* Pope Francis outlines and makes a very clear statement about the role of religious traditions as peacemakers. Such understanding of dialogue within and as an extension of the common good in the public sphere had already been prominent in his pontificate, and it came to fruition with the document on 'Human Fraternity for World Peace and Living Together' signed in Abu Dhabi on 4 February 2019.[74] In that sense, *FT* was an extension and development of such human fraternity between Christians and Muslims and effectively implemented in another journey outside Europe, Pope Francis' visit to Iraq in March 2021.[75] However, those visits to Abu Dhabi and Iraq became public catalysts of Pope Francis' role as peacemaker, and they were expressions of his convictions that religions exist for the service of fraternity in the world.[76]

Thus, different religions for Pope Francis 'contribute significantly to building fraternity and defending justice in society'.[77] Dialogue between those religions is central, but the reason for such dialogue to emerge is not necessarily one of diplomatic tolerance. Instead, 'the goal of dialogue is to establish friendship, peace, and harmony, and to share spiritual and moral values and experiences in a spirit of truth and love'.[78] For Pope Francis, openness to God is central to such justification of dialogue as reason only is not able to establish fraternity.[79] Indeed, it is through a transcendent truth that religions are able to adhere to just and fair relations between peoples, as self-interests together with class, group, or nation 'set them in opposition to one another'.[80] Religions have the capacity of contributing to the good of society when they acknowledge other human beings as 'travelling companions, truly brothers and sisters'.[81] As a result, the Church 'does not restrict her mission to the private sphere' while acknowledging the autonomy of political life.[82] In building a better world, not only taking part in charitable organisations, the Church also works 'for the advancement of humanity and of universal fraternity'.[83] The Church 'is a home with open doors, because she is a mother'.[84] As such the Church meets leaders of the world in order to promote and advocate peace and understanding, a common humanity and a common house, and the common purpose of religious traditions, as explored within the next chapter.

Notes

1 Apostolic Journey of His Holiness Pope Francis to Romania (31 May–2 June 2019), Meeting with the Authorities, with Civil Society and with the Diplomatic Corps, 'Address of His Holiness', Uniri Hall of the Cotroceni Palace (Bucharest), Friday 31 May 2019. Vatican City: Librería Editrice Vaticana.

2 Code of Canon Law § 112 calls all rites 'autonomous ritual Churches'. Those churches include the main six rites in which churches are included *sui iuris*: Latin Rite (Roman Catholic Church), Alexandrian Rite (Coptic Catholic Church, Eritrean Catholic Church, Ethiopian Catholic Church), West Syrian or Antiochene Rite (Maronite Catholic Church, Syriac Catholic Church, and Syro-Malankara Catholic Church), Armenian Rite (Armenian Catholic Church), East Syrian or Chaldean Rite (Chaldean Catholic Church and Syro-Malabar Catholic Church), Constantinopolitan or Byzantine Rite (Albanian Catholic Church, Belarusian Catholic Church, Bulgarian Greek Catholic Church, Byzantine Church of Croatia, Serbia and Montenegro or Križevci Catholic Church), and Greek Byzantine Catholic Church (Hungarian Greek Catholic Church, Italo-Albanian Catholic Church, Macedonian Catholic Church, Melkite Greek Catholic Church, Romanian Catholic Church, Ruthenian Catholic Church known as the Byzantine Catholic Church in America, Slovak Catholic Church, and Ukrainian Greek Catholic Church).

3 'Address of His Holiness', Uniri Hall of the Cotroceni Palace (Bucarest), Friday 31 May 2019.

4 Encyclical Letter *Lumen Fidei* of the Supreme Pontiff Francis to the Bishops, Priests, and Deacons Consecrated Persons and the Lay Faithful on Faith. Vatican City: Librería Editrice Vaticana, 2013.

5 The Year of Faith concluded with a Mass presided by Pope Francis at St Peter's Square on Sunday 24 November 2013.

6 *LF* § 7.
7 Holy Mass for the Conclusion of the Year of Faith on the Solemnity of Our Lord Jesus Christ, King of the Universe, 'Homily of Pope Francis', St Peter's Square, Sunday 24 November 2013 § 2. Vatican City: Librería Editrice Vaticana, 2013.
8 Dogmatic Constitution on the Church *Lumen Gentium* solemnly promulgated by His Holiness Pope Paul VI on 21 November 1964, Chapter II: On the People of God.
9 *Encyclical Letter Laudato Si' of the Holy Father Francis on Care for Our Common Home.* Vatican City: Librería Editrice Vaticana, 24 May 2015.
10 Fernando Chica Arellano and Carlos Granados García, eds. *Loado seas mi Señor: Comentario a la encíclica Laudato Si' del papa Francisco.* Madrid: Biblioteca de Autores Cristianos, 2015.
11 Austen Ivereigh, *Wounded Shepherd: Pope Francis and His Struggle to Convert the Catholic Church.* New York: Henry Holt and Company, 2019, p. 203.
12 Francis of Assisi, 'Canticle of the Creatures', in Regis J. Armstrong, O.F.M. Cap., J.A. Wayne Hellmann, O.F.M. Conv., and William J. Short, O.F.M., eds. *Francis of Assisi: Early Documents*, vol. I. New York, London, and Manila: New City Press, 1999, pp. 113–114.
13 *LS* § 10; on St Francis LS § 10–12.
14 *LS* § 1.
15 *LS* § 2.
16 *LS* § 2.
17 *LS* § 4.
18 *LS* §3. One would assume that Pope Francis in his inclusion would also include in this message the LGBTI community.
19 John XXIII, Apostolic Letter *Octogesima Adveniens*, 14 May 1971 § 21.
20 John XXIII, 'Address to FAO on the 25th Anniversary of Its Institution', 16 November 1970 § 4.
21 John Paul II, Encyclical Letter *Redemptor Hominis*, 4 March 1979, § 15.
22 John Paul II, *Catechesis*, 17 January 2001, § 4.
23 LS § 5, John Paul II, *Encyclical Letter Centesimus Annus*, 1 May 1991, § 38.
24 LS § 6, Benedict XVI, 'Address to the Diplomatic Corps Accredited to the Holy See', 8 January 2007, § 73.
25 LS § 7.
26 LS § 8, and Ecumenical Patriarch Bartholomew, 'Address in Santa Barbara, California, 8 November 1997', in John Chryssavgis, ed., *On Earth as in Heaven: Ecological Vision and Initiatives of Ecumenical Patriarch Bartholomew*, New York: Fordham University Press, 2011.

27 LS § 9, and Ecumenical Patriarch Bartholomew, 'Global responsibility and ecological sustainability', Closing Remarks, Halki Summit I, Istanbul, 20 June 2012.
28 LS § 13.
29 'Pope Francis gifts Fidel Castro with copy of Laudato Si', Catholic News Agency 20 September 2015 at Pope Francis gifts Fidel Castro with copy of 'Laudato Si' (catholicnewsagency.com), accessed 23 January 2021.
30 'Y lo mismo vemos también en Occidente, donde crece constantemente la distancia entre pobres y ricos y se produce una inquietante degradación de la dignidad personal con la droga, el alcohol y los sutiles espejismos de felicidad', Benedict XVI, Conferencia de Aparecida, 'Discurso inaugural de Su Santidad Benedicto XVI', § 4, 'Los problemas sociales y políticos'.
31 *LS* § 61 cited by Pope Francis in Apostolic Journey of His Holiness Pope Francis to Cuba, to the United States of America and visit to the United Nations Headquarters (19–28 September 2015), Visit to the Joint Session of the United States Congress, 'Address of the Holy Father', United States Capitol, Washington, DC, Thursday 24 September 2015. Vatican City: Librería Editrice Vaticana.
32 *Evangelii Gaudium* § 55 in Visit of His Holiness Pope Francis to the European Parliament and to the Council of Europe, 'Address of Pope Francis to the European Parliament', Strasbourg, France, Tuesday, 25 November 2014. Vatican City: Librería Editrice Vaticana.
33 Ivereigh, *Wounded Shepherd*, p. 219.
34 *LS* § 17.
35 *LS* § 18.
36 *LS* I, § 22.
37 *LS* § 23, 25.
38 *LS* II 'The issue of water', § 27.
39 *LS* § 32.
40 *LS* § 44.
41 *LS* § 52.
42 *LS* § 54.
43 *LS* Chapter 2: The Gospel of Creation.
44 Encyclical Letter *Fratelli Tutti* of the Holy Father Francis on Fraternity and Social Friendship. Vatican City: Librería Editrice Vaticana, 3 October 2020.
45 Elise Ann Allen, 'In first trip since COVID, pope visits Assisi to sign new encyclical', *Crux* 3 October 2020 (cruxnow.com), accessed 31 January 2021.
46 *FT* § 128.
47 *FT* § 129.
48 *FT* § 129.
49 *FT* § 130.

50 Visit to Lampedusa, 'Homily of Holy Father Francis', "Arena" sports camp, Salina Quarter, Monday 8 July 2013. Vatican City: Librería Editrice Vaticana.

51 Visit of the Holy Father to Bari for the meeting of reflection and spirituality, 'Mediterranean: Frontier of Peace', 23 February 2020, see *Bulletin of the Holy See Press Office*, 21 January 2020 at Visit of the Holy Father to Bari for the meeting of reflection and spirituality, "Mediterranean: frontier of peace" (23 February 2020–programme) (vatican.va), accessed 31 January 2021.

52 Visit of the Holy Father to Bari for the meeting of reflection and spirituality, 'Mediterranean: Frontier of Peace', Meeting with Bishops of the Mediterranean, 'Address of His Holiness', Basilica of St. Nicholas (Bari), Sunday, 23 February 2020. Vatican City: Librería Editrice Vaticana.

53 Visit of the Holy Father to Bari for the meeting of reflection and spirituality, 'Mediterranean: Frontier of Peace', Holy Mass, 'Homily of His Holiness', Bari, 23 February 2020. Vatican City: Librería Editrice Vaticana.

54 *FT* § 131.

55 Document '*On Human Fraternity for World Peace and Living Together*', Abu Dhabi, 4 February 2019, and *L'Osservatore Romano*, 4–5 February 2019, p. 7.

56 *FT* § 132.

57 *FT* § 133.

58 *FT* § 138 cf. Benedict XVI, Encyclical Letter *Caritas in Veritatis*, 29 June 2009 § 67.

59 *FT* § 138–139.

60 *FT* § 139.

61 *FT* § 140

62 *Gospel according to Matthew* 5:45, 6:3-4, 10:8.

63 *FT* § 141.

64 *FT* § 141.

65 *FT* Chapter 8.

66 *FT* § 255–270.

67 *FT* § 260.

68 *FT* § 261.

69 *FT* § 262.

70 Pope Francis, 'Message to the United Nations Conference to Negotiate a Legally Binding Instrument to Prohibit Nuclear Weapons', 28 March 2017, Vatican City: Librería Editrice Vaticana, and Paul VI, *Populorum Progressio*, 28 March 1967, § 51 and Journey to India, 'Address of Paul VI to the Press', Bombay, 4 December 1964, Vatican City: Librería Editrice Vaticana.

71 John Paul II, *Evangelium Vitae*: To the Bishops, Priests and Deacons, Men and Women Religious, Lay Faithful and all the People of

Good Will on the Value and Inviolability of Human Life, 25 March 1995, Vatican City: Librería Editrice Vaticana, and added to the *Catechism of the Catholic Church* § 2267.

72 *FT* § 263, and Pope Francis 'Address on the Twenty-fifth Anniversary of the Promulgation of the Catechism of the Catholic Church', 11 October 2017. Vatican City: Librería Editrice Vaticana. See also *Catechism of the Catholic Church*, second edition. Revised in accordance with the official Latin text promulgated by John Paul II. Includes revisions of paragraph no. 2267 promulgated by Pope Francis, Vatican City: Librería Editrice Vaticana, 2020.

73 Congregation for the Doctrine of the Faith, 'Letter to the Bishops Regarding the Revision of No. 2267 of the Catechism of the Catholic Church on the Death Penalty', 1 August 2018, *L'Osservatore Romano*, 3 August 2018, p. 8.

74 His Holiness Pope Francis and The Grand Imam of Al-Azhar Ahmed el-Tayeb, 'A Document on Human Fraternity for World Peace and Living Together', Abu Dhabi, 4 February 2019. Vatican City: Librería Editrice Vaticana.

75 'Apostolic Journey of His Holiness Francis in Iraq (5 to 8 March 2021) – Programme 08.02.2021', *Summary of Bulletin, Holy See Press Office*, 8 February 2021.

76 *FT* Chapter 8.

77 *FT* § 271.

78 Catholic Bishops' Conference of India, 'Response of the Church in India to the Present-day Challenges', 9 March 2016.

79 *FT* § 272.

80 *FT* § 273, cf. John Paul II, Encyclical Letter *Centecimus Annus*, 1 May 1991.

81 *FT* § 274.

82 *FT* § 276.

83 *FT* § 276, and Benedict XVI, Encyclical Letter *Caritas in Veritatis*, 29 June 2009.

84 *FT* § 276 and Pope Francis, 'Address to the Catholic Community, Rakovski, Bulgaria', 6 May 2019, *L'Osservatore Romano*, 8 May 2019, p. 9.

5

TOWARDS A SHARED
HUMANITY

In July 2013 (22–29) Pope Francis journeyed to Rio de Janeiro, Brazil to attend the celebrations of the 28th World Youth Day. That journey had been agreed by Benedict XVI before his resignation, and his invitation to the world youth to meet with him, dated 18 October 2012, had been a direct and welcoming call to the youth of Latin America, recalling the message of the bishops at Aparecida in 2007 to carry out a continental mission.[1] Pope Francis had been one of the central figures in the Latin American bishops' meetings at Aparecida; therefore, it was truly fitting that Archbishop Bergoglio of Buenos Aires reborn as Pope Francis would visit Brazil to meet with the youth of the world. The occasion was important for Pope Francis and therefore the possibility of a Plenary Indulgence was granted to those attending the meeting.[2] During the journey from Rome, Pope Francis was welcomed by very seasoned journalists, and he outlined his own understanding of contemporary youth belonging: 'they belong in all sorts of ways, and we must not isolate them! But in particular, we must not isolate them from the whole of society!'[3]

The meeting with the world youth had several undertones in which Pope Francis spelled out future aspects of his pontificate. Some of those foundational discourses were marked by his pastoral experiences in Latin America and particularly by the influence of his own contribution to the Aparecida meeting of Latin American bishops in 2007.[4] If one analyses several of the messages he gave in his visits outside Italy, and particularly at faraway places, it can be seen that Pope Francis expanded on these

DOI: 10.4324/9781003172345-6

early messages in Brazil. Such foundational pastoral lines could be considered syntheses of his own portfolio taken for granted by him that became lineaments for all his future visits and his leadership of the Roman Catholic Church. Thus, his address to the leadership of the Episcopal Conferences of Latin America has a down-to-earth, concrete, and clear agenda: a missionary discipleship 'is the journey which God desires for the present "today"', so that 'every utopian (future-oriented) or restorationist (past-oriented) impulse is spiritually unhealthy'.[5]

The dangers for the Christian journey were spelled out in Pope Francis' journey to Brazil and became his trademark, dangers to a missionary conversion that impede the process of discerning the present, namely making the Gospel an ideology. As a result of such isolated ideology, interpreting the Gospel without the community of the Church, a sociological reductionism that involves an interpretive claim that comes from the social sciences, including marker liberalism and Marxist categorisation; psychologising, a process attached to elites that aims at self-awareness; the gnostic solution that looks at a higher spirituality, disembodied thoughts of 'enlightened Catholics'; the Pelagian solution that seeks to return to the past; functionalism that focuses on fixing administrative processes and that makes the Church into an NGO; and, finally, clericalism, a common phenomenon in Latin America whereby the priest is exalted to the point that he is a higher human being rather than a servant for the world and the sacraments within the Christian community.[6]

Pope Francis' return to Latin America through Brazil opened one of the developments of his address to the Latin American bishops in Rio de Janeiro in 2013 that resonated with several countries: a common and global Amazonia. He returned to continue his journey with all those local churches that were working within such region and where indigenous populations were the majority. Thus, in July 2015, Pope Francis returned to Latin America for his visit to Ecuador, Bolivia, and Paraguay (5–13 July 2015).[7] During that visit, he had the opportunity to share time and to listen to concerns from the indigenous populations who at that time were the recipients of unstable political processes. Indeed, in his address to delegates of the Second World

Meeting of Popular Movements, he asked the question: 'What can I do, a farmwife, a native woman, a fisher who can hardly fight the domination of the big corporations?'[8] Such concerns were reaffirmed when Pope Francis visited Mexico in 2016 (12–18 February 2016), and he started engaging with the pastoral reality of indigenous populations not only when he visited Chiapas but also in his warm words to the Mexican bishops: 'I ask you to show singular tenderness in the way you regard indigenous peoples, them and their fascinating but not infrequently decimated cultures', reminding them that 'the indigenous peoples of Mexico still await true recognition of the richness of their contribution and the fruitfulness of their presence'.[9]

Prophetic bishops had led people there during difficult moments of affirmation of indigenous identity and guerrilla warfare during colonial times and in the 1990s. Thus, Bartolomé de las Casas had fought for the recognition of indigenous populations as human beings in the sixteenth century, and Bishop Samuel Ruiz García had supported indigenous rights during his long years as shepherd of Chiapas (1960–2000).[10] In Chiapas and at the meeting with representatives of the indigenous populations at the Municipal Sport Centre of Chiapas, Pope Francis told them clearly 'you have much to teach us, much to teach humanity. Your peoples, as the bishops of Latin América have recognised, know how to interact harmoniously with nature, which they respect as a "source of food, a common home and an altar of human sharing".[11] However, the pope's assurance came from his own words in Laudato Si': 'We rejoice in the certainty that "The Creator does not abandon us; he never forsakes his loving plan or repents of having created us".'[12]

It is such shared creation, co-creation, and care for the planet that Pope Francis brings not only to the Document on Human Fraternity but also to the concerns within Amazonia. Since the times of a young Bishop Pedro Casaldáliga and his spirituality of liberation together with his life in Amazonia, the Catholic Church has clashed with landlords, mining companies, logging companies, cattle ranchers, and with the Brazilian President Jair Bolsonaro. Is the Amazonia a patrimony of humanity and therefore a vast land to be protected, or is it just part of the state of Brazil and therefore a land to be sold and used according to economic policies? The uncontrolled fires of Amazonia caused a bridge between President Bolsonaro and the European Union, and indeed with the Vatican, conflict in which Pope Francis took central stage.

It was in that context that a Synod of Amazonia was fostered by Pope Francis in the ecclesial spirit of synodality to reflect on the possible responses to change and the awareness of a common home by pastoral agents living and working in Amazonia. The Synod's final document and Pope Francis' Apostolic Exhortation *Querida Amazonia* secured a clear and incisive global response not only to the efforts of the Church in the Amazonian region but also to the development of an integral ecology.[13] Such localised reflection became a renewed cry for inculturation and the integration of indigenous populations within the wisdom of the life of the Church so that 'for the Church to achieve a renewed inculturation of the Gospel in the Amazon region, she needs to listen to its ancestral wisdom, listen once more to the voice of its elders, recognise the values present in the way of life of the original communities, and recover the rich stories of its peoples'.[14]

Pope Francis' call was a profound appreciation of indigenous populations comparable to that of Paul VI in Kampala, Uganda in 1968 when he encouraged Africans to develop an African Christianity in a postcolonial era. Within those gifts already present in Amazonia he rescued the interconnection and interdependence of creation, and the mysticism of graciousness that loves life as a gift, 'the mysticism of a sacred wonder before nature and all its forms of life'.[15] Pope Francis broke with the cautiousness regarding indigenous institutions and indigenous metaphysics of John Paul II and Benedict XVI when he returned to the support by Paul VI of divine processes of inculturation so that Pope Francis asserted that 'inculturation elevates and fulfils'.[16] For the mission, dialogue, intercultural support, and acceptance were of the essence to the role of the Church in Amazonia so that 'in an Amazonian region characterized by many religions, we believers need to find occasions to speak to one another and to act together for the common good and the promotion of the poor'.[17]

The world pandemic of COVID-19 interrupted journeys and movements, and Pope Francis stressed the communion by the Church with other religions as well as with the world. Pope Francis, the peacemaker, was called to address the world as a parish priest would do it, but his desire to go to Iraq was stronger than any fear of the pandemic. Thus, once the Vatican residents were all vaccinated, he reaffirmed his wish to go to Iraq, completing a full cycle of eight years affirming victims and making concrete efforts to foster and push for international peace and global understanding.

From Lampedusa to Baghdad

The pope from the ends of the world started his journey of a peacemaker after his election in March 2013 with a trip to Lampedusa in July 2013, an occasion in which his message of peace between migrants and the European Union was reaffirmed. It continued with a sustained peacemaking between inhabitants of the planet; the planet as a coexistent home for all – humans, animals, nature. Such interdependence on the centrality of a human fraternity was actualised in Abu Dhabi in February 2019 through the signing of the Document on Human Fraternity by Christians and Muslims with less peacemaking activities in person during the world pandemic of 2020. However, as soon as it was possible, Pope Francis decided to plan a visit to those Christians who had seen years of war, Islamic terrorism, and crimes against humanity in Iraq (March 2021).[18] After his visit to Iraq, he confided with others that his awareness of Iraq and the need to visit them were triggered by one single book – *The Last Girl*, the memoirs as a victim of Daesh by the Yazidi Nobel Prize winner Nadia Murad.[19] Nadia Murad narrates the immediate past and her history within the Yazidi of 2014 in Iraq. Daesh tried to exterminate the Yazidi with a previous 'rational' application of a horrible logic of genocide which has been summarised by Nadia Murad's barrister: Yazidi for Daesh are not believers and therefore they can be enslaved.[20] ISIS attacked Nadia Murad's village, and she was sold as a slave. ISIS prepared the Yazidi genocide through their 'Research and Fatwa Department' that studied the

Yazidis and concluded that as a Kurdish-speaking group they did not have a holy book and therefore as nonbelievers they were to be enslaved as an extension of the Sharia.[21] ISIS produced a written guideline on slaves and prisoners called *Questions and Answers on Taking Captives and Slaves*.[22] Within that vade mecum, horrible questions were asked: 'Is it permissible to have intercourse with the female slave who has not reached puberty?' The answer was positive, if she is fit for intercourse; 'Is it permissible to sell a female captive?' The answer was positive, because they are merely property.[23]

In her Nobel Lecture, Nadia Murad moved from a personal testimony to represent all Yazidi women in her public request for justice.[24] Her testimony was about the significant change experienced by the Yazidi community as a result of ISIS's genocide on part of the community of Iraq by making women into slaves, killing men, and further by the destruction of Yazidi's pilgrimage sites and houses of worship. For Nadia Murad, that day in Oslo when she received the Nobel Prize was a very special one, not only for her but also for all Yazidi because 'humanity defeated terrorism', and it was the triumph of women and their children over the perpetrators of crimes against the Yazidi. For her, the hope of the start of peace negotiations was central to her lecture, the start of the protection of women, children, and minorities, especially victims of sexual violence. She recalled her dreams of normality and family life, before ISIS killed her mother, six of her brothers, and her brothers' children. According to her understanding, ISIS wanted to eradicate their religion which had provided peaceful lives and a society of tolerance for a long time. Iraq, Kurdistan, and the international community did not protect them, and while they sympathised with the Yazidi the genocide did not stop, and she maintained that such threat of annihilation is still present. The Yazidi remained in camps, and their villages have not been rebuilt while the perpetrators of the killings remain at large.

Such narrative convinced Pope Francis that he should head for Iraq, a wish that had been denied to John Paul II who was advised not to visit because of security concerns. The danger that Pope Francis undertook in his visit to Iraq cannot be underestimated, particularly when attacks on government buildings were still taking place but within a world closed to international travel because of the pandemic. Before his visit he spoke about his non-fear of death and the closeness and support he wanted to bring to Iraqi Christians. Indeed, one could argue that the closeness with Churches of the East came through his deep affection for Patriarch Bartholomew of Constantinople. The week before the visit, he increased the centrality of other rites apart from the Latin Church by signing the decree that established the liturgical feast of Saint Gregory of Narek on 27 February.[25] Gregory of Narek was an Armenian mystical and lyric poet, a monk and a theologian venerated in the Armenian and Catholic Churches who was declared Doctor of the Church by Pope Francis in 2017 (born Rashtunik, Turkey, 951 died in Narekavank, Turkey in 1003). In addition to the Mass held at St Peter's, an Ecumenical Prayer was celebrated at the statue of St Gregory of Narek blessed by Pope Francis in the Vatican Gardens in 2018. The Ecumenical Prayer was presided by His Eminence Archbishop Khajag Barsamian, the representative of the Armenian Apostolic Church in Rome, in the presence of His Eminence Cardinal Kurt Koch, the President of the Pontifical Council for Promoting Christian Unity.[26]

Those preparations for Iraq were marked by the Spiritual Exercises for the Roman Curia which were not undertaken in person but with personal arrangements for personal prayer, with the suspension of all Pope Francis' engagements, including the General Audience of 24 February 2021.[27] Lenten Sermons were delivered by Cardinal Raniero Cantalamessa O.F.M. Cap, Preacher of the Papal Household, his first sermon concerning Christological dogma and Matthew 16:15.[28] A few days prior to his journey to Iraq, Pope Francis delivered a video message in which he reiterated his wish to visit and meet the people of Iraq as a penitent pilgrim of peace. He told them: 'I am coming as a pilgrim, as a *penitent pilgrim*, to implore from the Lord forgiveness and reconciliation after years of war and terrorism, to beg from God the consolation of hearts and the healing of wounds. I am coming among you also as a *pilgrim of peace,* to repeat the words: You are all brothers and sisters' (Matthew 23:8).[29] It was clear that the visit was confirmed not by videos or press conferences but by the customary visit by Pope Francis to the Basilica Santa Maria

Maggiore where the venerated image of Salus Populi Romano is located, depicting the Blessed Virgin Mary as the health and protectress of the Roman people which was granted a Canonical coronation by Pope Gregory XVI on 15 August 1838 (Papal Bull *Caelestis Regina*).

Pope Francis's visit to Iraq was marked by the possibility of peace and stability in a post-pandemic Iraq where Christians and those who had suffered under ISIS could once again be made to feel as citizens rather than protected minorities in Iraq. His visit was marked by the conversations with the Iraqi authorities and the affirmation of existence to Christian leaders and catechists at the Siro-Catholic Cathedral of 'Our Lady of Salvation' in Baghdad. It must be remembered that Pope Francis has never supported the use of the term 'minorities' used globally but that he had requested equal rights and human dignity for all human beings within the states in which they reside.

Pope Francis' visit to Grand Ayatollah Sayyid Ali Al-Husayni Al-Sistani in Najaf marked the continuation of good relations and a shared human fraternity between Christians and Muslims. Ayatollah Sistani was at that time one of the most influential Iraqi Shia marja' (source to follow) of Iranian origins living in Iraq. Born in Mashhad in a family of religious clerics that claim descent from Husayn ibn Ali, the grandson of Muhammad. In 2006, Ayatollah Sistani had been nominated for the Nobel Peace Prize by Iraqi Christians, and, in the subsequent years, he was also acknowledged as an important player in peace negotiations in Iraq by Western commentators and a worthy nominee for the Nobel Prize. The images of that day were moving and clear: Pope Francis was walking the narrow streets to reach Al Sistani's house, and the Grand Ayatollah welcomed him personally sharing a close moment of intimacy that sent clear signals to the Shia community that peace was on the horizon.

Such contribution by Pope Francis and Ayatollah Sistani was also marked by an interreligious meeting on the plains of Ur, after the pope's arrival in Nasiriya. The opening lines by Pope Francis were remarkably timely: 'This blessed place brings us back to our origins, to the sources of God's work, to the birth of our religions'.[30] Furthermore, Pope Francis outlined the future by looking back at Abraham's actions: 'We look up to heaven. Thousands of years later, as we look up to the same sky, those same stars appear. They illumine the darkest nights because they shine together. Heaven thus imparts a message of unity: the Almighty above invites us never to separate ourselves from our neighbours'.[31]

The diversity of the rites and Christian communities present in Iraq was shown by Pope Francis' celebration of the Eucharist at the Chaldean Cathedral of 'Saint Joseph' in Baghdad. On the following day, Pope Francis visited the Autonomous Region of Iraqi Kurdistan; he had a meeting with the government as well as attended several landmark events reached by helicopter, including a 'Prayer of Suffrage for the Victims of the War' at Hosh al-Bieaa (Church Square) in Mosul, a visit to the Qaraqosh Community at the Church of 'Immaculate Conception' in Qaragosh, and the public celebration of the Eucharist at the 'Franso Hariri' Stadium in Erbil. These were towns and communities where Daesh had clearly attempted to exterminate non-Muslims and those Muslims who were perceived as non-Muslims such as the Yazidi. In Mosul, Daesh fighters had proclaimed the existence of the caliphate on 13 June 2014, and they had sworn to reach Rome in their fight for a unified militant Islam under Daesh.[32] A newly sectarian governance system was put into place with new education curricula, the sale of women, and a militant Islam whose followers did not have a place for diversity or other religions.[33]

The previous day a group of interested parties and scholars of Iraq had a meeting, hosted online, with Omar Mohammed of the Mosul Eye. The meeting addressed Omar's sense that the Pope's visit could be the last chance to put the reconstruction and the suffering accumulated in Mosul to the Iraqi government and the international community.[34] I was more hopeful, and so I made it clear at that meeting.[35] Indeed, one of the characteristics of a papal visit relates to the fact that crowds come out to see a pope and then they return to their own lives and activities. However, at the level of state and church, there are continuities because of the ongoing diplomatic relations between the Vatican and the different states as well as the pastoral objectives and plans by local churches re-discussed through the bishops' periodic *ad limina* visit to Rome to discuss pending and pressing issues with the different popes.[36]

However, Pope Francis did not disappoint when he visited Mosul. He led a prayer for fraternity and condemned violence and sectarianism in the name of religion. However, he took longer than anticipated and made a small tour of the Mosul destruction, looking very fragile and touched by such destruction. Pope Francis' words introducing his prayer for those who had been killed at Mosul, and in war, were clear and firm:

> Today, however, we reaffirm our conviction that fraternity is more durable than fratricide, that hope is more powerful than hatred, that peace more powerful than war. This conviction speaks with greater eloquence than the passing voices of hatred and violence, and it can never be silenced by the blood spilled by those who pervert the name of God to pursue paths of destruction.[37]

And Pope Francis' theological reasoning was clear and he made it public:

> If God is the God of life – for so he is – then it is wrong for us to kill our brothers and sisters in his Name. If God is the God of peace – for so he is – then it is wrong for us to wage war in his Name. If God is the God of love – for so he is – then it is wrong for us to hate our brothers and sisters.[38]

During the same day, Pope Francis paid a visit to the Qaraqosh Community at the Church of the 'Immaculate Conception' in Qaragosh. Pope Francis praised their joy and diversity and encouraged those present with the following instruction: 'Dream!' They were beautiful words followed by the hope of the heavenly and earthly examples:

> Do not give up! Do not lose hope! From heaven the saints are watching over us. Let us pray to them and never tire of begging their intercession. There are also the saints

next-door, "who, living in our midst, reflect God's presence".[39] This land has many of them, because it is a land
of many holy men and women. Let them accompany you
to a better future, a future of hope.

Pope Francis' pastoral visit ended with the celebration of the
Eucharist at the 'Franso Hariri' Stadium in Erbil where in a
very joyful atmosphere Iraqis of state and church were able to
celebrate.

On return to Rome and during his catechesis of 19 March
2021, Pope Francis confessed that his soul was full of gratitude
to God and to all those who made it possible, state and religious
authorities, beginning, in the words of Pope Francis, 'with the
Grand Ayatollah Al-Sistani, with whom I had an unforgettable
meeting in his residence in Najaf'.[40]

Conclusions: a shepherd's desire for peace and closeness

Pope Francis' desire to support those at the peripheries of the
world has been the characteristic of his pontificate. For a pope
coming from the ends of the world has not forgotten the struggles
of injustice and inequality suffered at the peripheries but has also
taken the Catholic Church with him. Thus, Amazonia has been
important for his global-centred ecological issues and spirituality, a continuity of his own contribution at the Latin American
Bishops Conference in Aparecida, Brazil. The closeness of a shepherd was expressed by his phrase 'shepherds with sheep's smell'
and the virtual encounter with a globalised community through
his *Urbi et Orbi* prayer and blessing from St Peter's Square during the 2020 pandemic. Furthermore, his desire to visit Iraq in
March 2021 outlined his preoccupation for areas in which Christians had been marginalised and demonised by the extremist Is-
lamists such as Daesh, or by the military in Myanmar, extending
his preoccupation not only to Christians but also to the Muslim
Rohingya, and to indigenous populations in Amazonia and indeed throughout the world.[41] His desire to visit Iraq in 2021 was
the climax of a shepherd who tried not only to be a peacemaker

but that through vulnerability and fragility showed others that he cared for them, be they Christian communities or victims of ISIS and other totalitarian movements who acted criminally in the name of religion such as the military in Myanmar.

Synodality as a process of working together with the centre and from the peripheries has been a seal of communion between the Bishop of Rome as the centre of the universal Roman Catholic Church and with other Eastern Churches. And such synodality was implemented by the Synod of the Amazonia as well as the inclusion for the first time in history of a woman as undersecretary of the Synod of Bishops, with voting rights, and dressed without a veil. She is addressed as the Reverend Doctor Nathalie Becquart with studies of ecclesiology and research on synodality.[42] Her appointment marked a peacemaking inclusion exercise that followed a couple of years of enquiry by the commission on women deacons and the explorations on the ordination of married clergy by the Amazonian Synod. Indeed, Pope Francis the peacemaker acted as a mediator between those who wanted radical changes in the Catholic Church and the traditionalists who accused him of not adhering to doctrine in his welcoming of members of the LGBT community, separated and divorced, immigrants, members of other faiths, and women. A peacemaker in the global scene as well as a peacemaker within his own family.

As Pope Francis showed his normality, fragility, and vulnerability on his journey to Iraq in March 2021 I conclude this study of Pope Francis the peacemaker returning to such dialogue of peace that a person deeply human can carry out in the name of an incarnate God. In my first work on Pope Francis that covered his life journey from birth to papal election, I stressed his enduring simplicity recalling his conversation with journalists on his way from his trip to Brazil after attending the World Youth Meeting in July 2013. In an attempt to penetrate the 'mystery' of the black briefcase he carried with him, the journalists asked: 'what do you have in that black briefcase that you carry with you at all time?' No other pope had carried his own briefcase during his journeys. Pope Francis replied: 'I don't have the key to an atomic bomb. I carried it with me because I always did before. What was inside? The necessary tools to shave, a breviary, my diary, something to read – I brought a book by Saint Teresita, of whom I am a devotee. I always carried my briefcase myself during my journeys: it is a normal occurrence, and we must be normal!'[43] In conclusion one may say, for Pope Francis it has been normal to be a peacemaker all his life. Indeed, his briefcase has witnessed such a journey of a peacemaker assessed within this work in the period 2013–2021.

Notes

1 'Message of His Holiness Benedict XVI for the Twenty-Eight World Youth Day 2013', Vatican 18 October 2012. Vatican City: Librería Editrice Vaticana.

2 'Decree of the Apostolic Penitentiary according to which Special Indulgences are granted to the faithful on the occasion of the 28th World Youth Day, Rio de Janeiro, 22–29 July 2013', Rome, Seat of the Apostolic Penitentiary 24 June 2013.

3 Apostolic Journey to Rio de Janeiro on the occasion of the XXVIII World Youth Day, 'Meeting of the Holy Father Francis with the Journalists during the Flight to Brazil', Papal Flight, Monday, 22 July 2013. Vatican City: Librería Editrice Vaticana.

4 See the conclusions of the Aparecida meeting of Latin American Bishops at V Conferencia General del Episcopado Latinoamericano y del Caribe, 'Documento Conclusivo', Aparecida 13–31 mayo 2007, third edition, Bogotá: Centro de Publicaciones del CELAM, 2008.

5 Pope Francis' Apostolic Journey to Rio de Janeiro on the occasion of the XXVIII World Youth Day, 'Address to the Leadership of the Episcopal Conferences of Latin America during the General Coordination Meeting', Sumaré Study Center, Rio de Janeiro, Sunday 28 July 2013. Vatican City: Librería Editrice Vaticana.

6 'Address to the Leadership of the Episcopal Conferences of Latin America' § 4.1, 4.2 & 4.3.

7 'Apostolic Journey of His Holiness Pope Francis to Ecuador, Bolivia and Paraguay 5–13 July 2015'. Vatican City: Librería Editrice Vaticana.

8 Participation at the Second World Meeting of Popular Movements, 'Address of the Holy Father', Expo Feria Exhibition Centre, Santa Cruz de la Sierra (Bolivia), Thursday 9 July 2015, § 1. Vatican City: Librería Editrice Vaticana.

9 Meeting with the Bishops of Mexico, 'Address of His Holiness Pope Francis', Metropolitan Cathedral of the Assumption, Mexico City, Saturday 13 February 2016. Vatican City: Librería Editrice Vaticana.

10 Gustavo Gutiérrez, *Las Casas: In Search of the Poor of Jesus Christ*. Maryknoll, NY: Orbis, 1994, and Gary MacEoin, *The People's Church: Bishop Samuel Ruiz of Mexico and Why He Matters*. New York: Crossroad, 1996.

11 *Aparecida* § 472, and Apostolic Journey of His Holiness Pope Francis to Mexico (12–18 February 2016), 'Holy Mass with Representatives of the Indigenous Communities of Chiapas: Homily of His Holiness Pope Francis', Municipal Sport Centre, San Cristóbal de Las Casas, Monday 15 February 2016. Vatican City: Librería Editrice Vaticana.

12 *Laudato Si'* § 13.

13 Pope Francis, Post-Synodal Apostolic Exhortation *Querida Amazonía* of the Holy Father Francis to the People of God and to All Persons of Good Will. Chawton, Hampshire: Redemptorist Publications, 2020.

14 *Querida Amazonía* (QA) § 70.

15 QA § 73.

16 QA § 73.

17 QA § 106.

18 'Apostolic Journey of His Holiness Pope Francis to Iraq 5–8 March 2021' at Apostolic Journey to the Republic of Iraq (5–8 March 2021) | Francis (vatican.va).

19 Nadia Murad and Jenna Krajeski, *The Last Girl: My Story of Captivity and My Fight against the Islamic State*. London: Virago Press, 2017.

20 Amal Clooney, 'Foreword', in Nadia Murad, and Jenna Krajeski, *The Last Girl: My Story of Captivity and My Fight against the Islamic State*. London: Virago, 2017, ix–xi.

21 Amal Clooney, 'Foreword', in Nadia Murad, and Jenna Krajeski, *The Last Girl*, x.

22 Amal Clooney, 'Foreword', in Nadia Murad, and Jenna Krajeski, *The Last Girl*, x.

23 Amal Clooney, 'Foreword', in Nadia Murad, and Jenna Krajeski, *The Last Girl*, x.

24 © Nobel Lecture given by Nobel Peace Prize Laureate 2018, Nadia Murad, Oslo, 10 December 2018.

25 Press Release of the Congregation for the Eastern Churches and the Pontifical Council for Promoting Christian Unity 26.02.2021, 'First liturgical commemoration of Saint Gregory of Narek according to the Roman Calendar'.

26 Press Release of the Congregation for the Eastern Churches and the Pontifical Council for Promoting Christian Unity (vatican.va).

27 Holy See Press Office Communiqué, 'Conclusion of the Spiritual Exercises for the Roman Curia', 20 January 2021.

28 Cardinal Raniero Cantalamessa, 'But who do you say that I am?' (Matthew 16:15) – Christological dogma, font of light and

inspiration', First Sermon of Lent, 26.02.2021, *Summary of Bulletin Holy Press Office*, 26 February 2021.

29 'Video Message of the Holy Father Francis Prior to His Apostolic Journey to Iraq', 5–8 March 2021. Vatican City: Librería Editrice Vaticana.

30 Apostolic Journey to the Republic of Iraq: Interreligious meeting, 'Address of His Holiness', Plain of Ur, 6 March 2021. Vatican City: Librería Editrice Vaticana.

31 'Address of His Holiness', Plain of Ur, 6 March 2021.

32 Mosul Eye, 'Prefazione' in Laura Quadarella Sanfelice di Monteforte, *Vivere a Mosul con l'Islamic State: Efficienza e brutalitá del Califfato*. Preface by Mosul Eye. Ugo Mursia Editore, 2019.

33 Mathilde Becker Aarseth, *Mosul under ISIS: Eyewitness Accounts of Life in the Caliphate*. London: I.B. Tauris, 2021.

34 On the architectural destruction in Mosul by ISIS, see Karel Nováček, Miroslav Melčák, Ondřej Beránek, and Lenka Starková, *Mosul after Islamic State: The Quest for Lost Architectural Heritage*. New York: Palgrave Macmillan, 2021.

35 Mario I. Aguilar to Mosul Eye, 6 March 2021.

36 In the case of Iraq, see, for example, 'Address of His Holiness Pope Francis to Members of the Synod of Chaldean Church', Monday, 26 October 2015. Vatican City: Librería Editrice Vaticana.

37 Apostolic Journey of His Holiness Pope Francis to Iraq, 5–8 March 2021, 'Prayer of Suffrage for the Victims', Hosh al-Bieaa (Church Square) in Mosul', Sunday, 7 March 2021. Vatican City: Librería Editrice Vaticana.

38 'Prayer of Suffrage for the Victims', Hosh al-Bieaa (Church Square) in Mosul', Sunday, 7 March 2021.

39 *Apostolic Exhortation Gaudete et Exsultate of the Holy Father Francis on the Call to Holiness in Today's World*, § 7. Rome, 19 March 2018. Vatican City: Librería Editrice Vaticana.

40 Pope Francis, General Audience, 'Catechesis on the Apostolic Journey to Iraq', Library of the Apostolic Palace, Wednesday, 10 March 2021. Vatican City: Librería Editrice Vaticana.

41 Pope Francis confirmed his intention to visit Iraq during his meeting with a delegation from the Catholic News Service on 1st February 2021; see Holy See Press Office, 'Audience with a delegation from the "Catholic News Service", 01.02.2021' at Audience with a delegation from the "Catholic News Service" (vatican.va), accessed 6 February 2021.

42 Holy See Press Office, 'Resignations and Appointments 06.02.2021: Appointment of under-secretaries of the Synod of Bishops' at Resignations and Appointments (vatican.va), accessed 6 February 2021.

43 Mario I. Aguilar, *Pope Francis: His Life and Thought*. Cambridge: Lutterworth, 2014, p. 181.

INDEX